MANDOLIN GO

CW00537372

100+ OF THE MOST POPULAR SELECTIONS

ARRANGED FOR MANDOLIN

Dan Fox

Alfred

Copyright © MMII by Alfred Publishing Co., Inc.
All rights reserved.   Printed in USA.
ISBN 0-7390-2472-8

Contents

Foreword

Here is a collection of music for the mandolin, an instrument that for almost 300 years has charmed everyone from classical composers to bluegrass pickers, from the most virtuosic concert artists to modest amateurs. This cross-section of over 100 songs, solos, and concert pieces includes bluegrass, old-time fiddle tunes, classical music (including the complete solo mandolin part from Vivaldi's *Concerto in C Major*), folk songs from America, Ireland, the Jewish tradition and, of course, Italy, plus many others.

Most of the selections are well within the reach of the average player. To help those with less-developed music-reading skills, we have included four-line tablature as well as traditional music notation for every piece except a few of the classical selections. Many of the tunes include interesting variations and authentic-sounding fills as well as complete words and music.

A Short History of the Mandolin

The mandolin as we know it was first heard in the early 18th century. It developed out of a family of stringed instruments that included the *lute* (see below), the *cittern*, the *pandura* (see below), and especially the *mandola* or *mandora* of which it is a direct descendant. The precursor to all of these, the *Arabian lute* or *oud*, was brought to Europe by the Arabs probably as early as the eighth century. It had a pear-shaped back, a peg box at right angles to the neck and—like our mandolin—eight strings tuned in four pairs. It, too, was played with a pick or plectrum.

At first there were many different styles of mandolin, some having as many as six pairs of strings. The model that eventually crowded out the others was the Neapolitan mandolin with four pairs of strings tuned in unisons and having the following pitches (from low to high): G (below middle C), D, A, and E. The tuning was identical to that of the violin, allowing players of that instrument to "double" on mandolin.

Lute

Pandura

Chitarra Spagnola

Cittern

This contributed greatly to the immediate popularity of the mandolin, and soon composers of the stature of Vivaldi and Mozart were writing for it in some important works. (The mandolin parts to Vivaldi's *Concerto in C Major* and Mozart's charming accompaniment to the canzonetta from his opera *Don Giovanni* are found in this book.) George Frederic Handel (1685–1759) composed several works for the mandolin, and the Italian master Giovanni Paisiello (1740–1816) wrote a concerto that is still performed today.

In the 19th century both Beethoven and Berlioz wrote for the mandolin, and in the 20th century such modern giants as Gustav Mahler, Igor Stravinsky, and Arnold Schoenberg made new demands on it. But the main popularity of the mandolin has always been with ordinary people who love its sweet tone, easy portability, and comparatively low cost. By the early 1900s there were hundreds of mandolin orchestras throughout the world. These consisted of large sections of mandolins to play the orchestral parts usually assigned to the violins. A family of larger, double-stringed, fretted instruments rounded out the string sections: mandolas (not to be confused with the medieval mandola or mandora) for the viola parts, mandocellos for the cello parts, and the ungainly mandobass or sometimes a bass balalaika for the lowest parts. Some orchestras also included banjos and guitars, and others augmented the string sound with a small section of woodwinds. Although mandolin orchestras are not nearly as numerous as they once were, there are still many in existence in New York, Providence and other American cities, in Europe, and especially in Japan where the instrument is very popular.

The development of bluegrass has interested a whole new generation of musicians in the mandolin. Players such as Jesse McReynolds (of Jim and Jesse), Bobby Osborne (of the Osborne Brothers), and especially Bill Monroe developed the hard-driving style that we now call the bluegrass of the 1930s and 40s. It brought the mandolin—along with the fiddle and five-string banjo—up into the front line of the bluegrass combo and gave it an equal voice in the exciting ensemble playing as well as allowing plenty of room for solo flights. Contemporary pickers like Andy Statman and Sam Bush have continued this tradition and raised the instrument to new heights of virtuosity. Modern mandolinists often have wide-ranging interests.

•The word "mandolin" is derived from the Italian word for almond.

Jethro Burns (of Homer and Jethro), although from Tennessee, and country through and through, has a repertoire that includes jazz tunes by Count Basie, Duke Ellington and Neal Hefti. New Jersey-based virtuoso Barry Mitterhoff is as comfortable playing bluegrass as he is with klezmer (traditional Jewish music), an Italian ballad, or a classical concert piece.

Today virtually all mandolins are constructed either in the original bowl-backed Neapolitan style with a round or almond-shaped* sound hole, favored by classical and folk players, or the flat-back style with two *f*-shaped sound holes which most bluegrass and jazz players prefer. Some mandolinists place a pickup on the bridge so the instrument can be amplified, an absolute necessity if it is to be heard over the typical jazz or bluegrass band. There are solid-body mandolins on the market, and these also must be amplified to be heard. Nevertheless, the growing interest in acoustic music has revived the desire to hear the mandolin in its pure, unamplified form.

For this almost-300-year-old instrument the future looks bright. Bluegrass is more popular than ever. The concert repertoire is growing. Many musicians who play traditional Jewish music in klezmer bands are using it. Some Irish bands feature its sound. And mandolin orchestras continue to thrive throughout the world, playing the traditional repertoire as well as new works commissioned by them.

Mandola

Arkansas Traveler

For many years this tune and the comedy routine that went with it—the interplay between a city slicker and a country cousin—were staples of the vaudeville stage. You'll occasionally hear the tune played in old movies and cartoons to suggest a country bumpkin. Play this arrangement at a brisk tempo and follow the fingering carefully.

American Folk Song

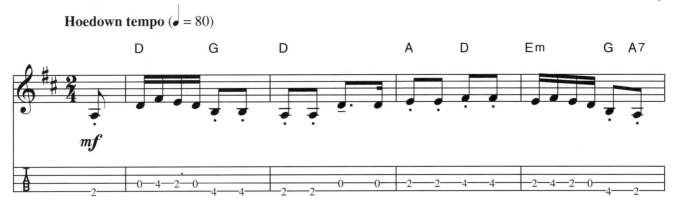

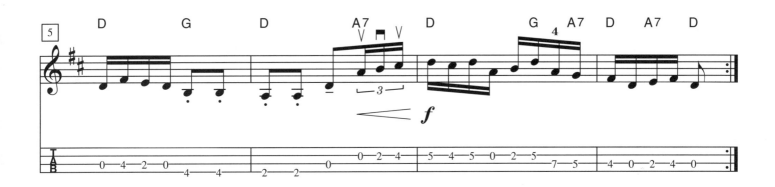

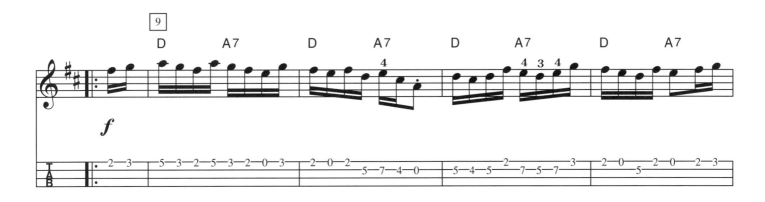

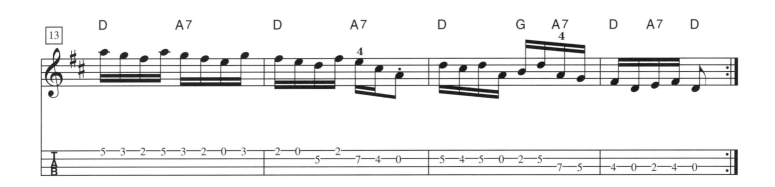

Banks of the Ohio

There is a long tradition of murder ballads that goes back to "Lord Randal," in England and includes "Tom Dooley" and "Pretty Polly" in America. This one has become a bluegrass standard. In this arrangement, the melody is often played below the open A string, which acts like the drone of a bagpipe or the unfingered 5th string on the five-string banjo. Use tremolo on all long notes.

American Folk Song

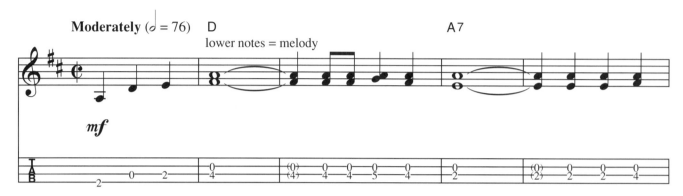

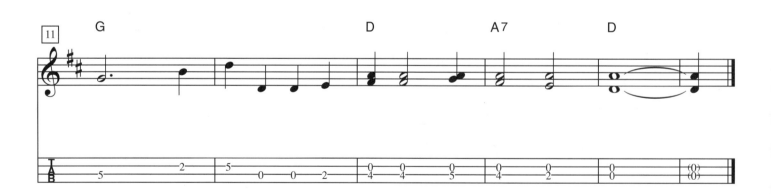

I asked my love to take a walk, to take a walk, a little walk,
Down beside where the waters flow, along the banks of the O-hi-o.

And only say that you'll be mine, and no other arms you'll find,
Down beside where the waters flow, along the banks of the O-hi-o.

Billy in the Lowland

This old-time fiddle tune is a staple of the bluegrass repertoire. Notice the fingering on the first four 16th notes in measure 3. Play them with alternate picking. Playing the first A on the 3rd string and the second A open avoids having to skip over a string after a downpick.

Old-time Fiddle Tune

Black-Eyed Susie

Playing the harmony above the melody adds a lot of excitement to this lively dance tune.
To make it easier to read, the melody is always stemmed downward in this arrangement.

American Folk Song

Verse:
All I want in this creation,
Is a pretty little wife on a big plantation.

Chorus:
Hey, little black-eyed Susie (3 times) Hey!

Verse:
Love my wife, I love my baby,
I love my biscuits sopped in gravy.
(repeat Chorus)

Cindy

When playing this bright country dance tune, pay close attention to the articulations. A staccato dot (·) over or under a note means to cut it off short. A tenuto dash (—) means to hold the note for its full value and give it a slight accent.

Traditional Country Song

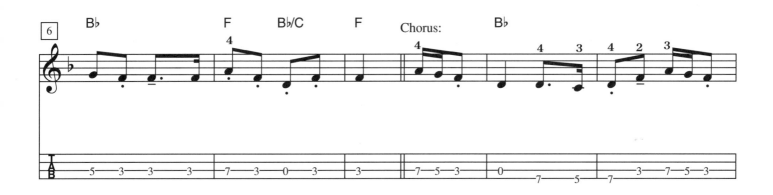

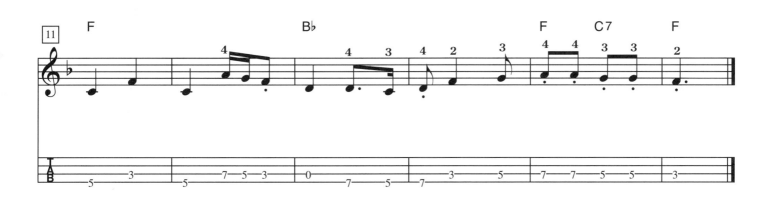

Verse:
You ought to see my Cindy,
She lives away down south.
Well, she's so sweet the honey bees,
Just swarm around her mouth.

Chorus:
Get along home, Cindy, Cindy,
Get along home, I say,
Get along home, Cindy, Cindy,
I'll marry you someday.

Coney in the Creek

A coney is a type of rabbit after which New York's "Coney Island" is named. The second strain of this tune is very reminiscent of "Turkey in the Straw." But, since the words of the song upon which "Turkey in the Straw" is based mentions it, we know that "Coney in the Creek" is the earlier melody.

Old-time Fiddle Tune

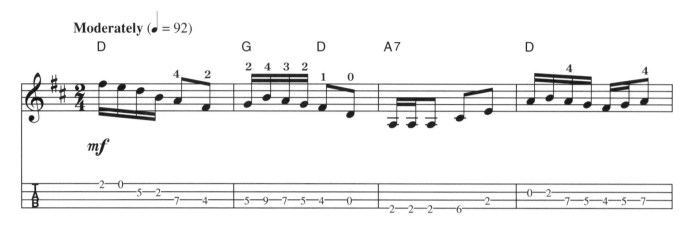

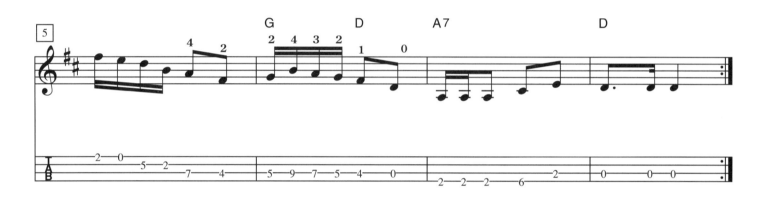

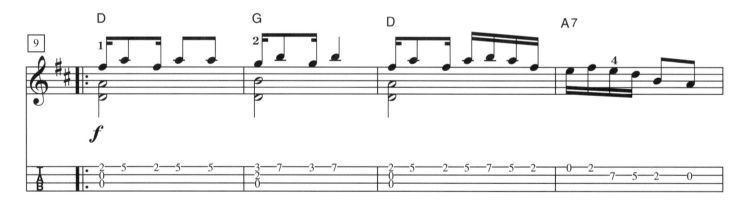

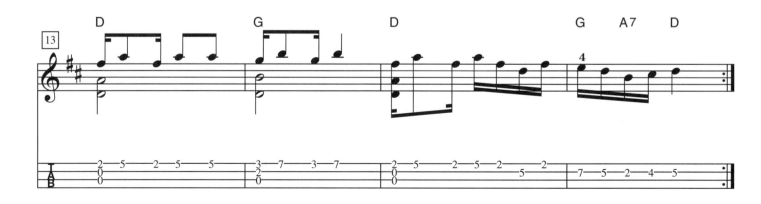

Fly Around, My Pretty Little Miss

This lively square dance tune probably originated in the Ozarks. Play it fast and rhythmic using alternate picking for the eighth notes.

American Dance Tune

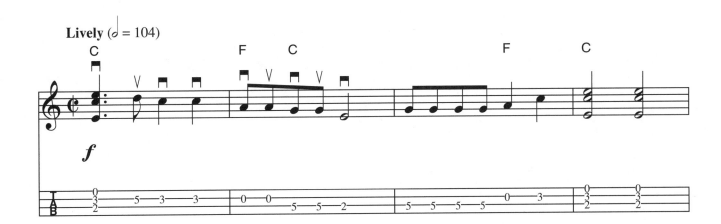

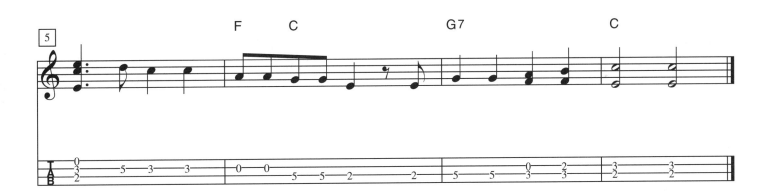

Fly around, my pretty little miss,
Fly around, my daisy.
Fly around, my pretty little miss,
You almost drive me crazy!

Coffee grows on white oak trees,
The river flows with brandy,
If I had my pretty little miss,
I'd feed her sugar candy.

Cripple Creek

This is one of the most famous of all country fiddle tunes. Always start the triplet pickups with an up-pick so you wind up with a downpick on the downbeat. Watch the fingering on the double-note slides: they are a very important part of this tune and must be brought out clearly.

Old-time Fiddle Tune

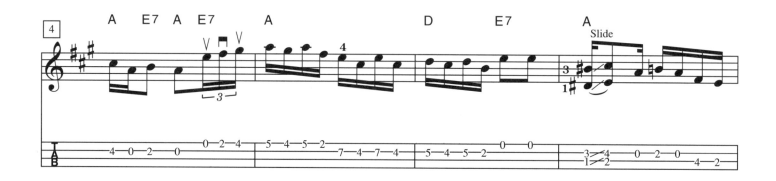

Good for the Wrist

Originally known as "Good for the Tongue," this is a tune that old-time fiddlers used to show off their technique. It makes a demanding technical exercise for mandolin, requiring a lot of crosspicking and fast fingering. The "Prepare barre" instruction means to finger the F and B♭ simultaneously by placing the 1st finger across the 1st and 2nd strings. This avoids the awkwardness of playing the F and then having to raise the 1st finger and move it back to the 2nd string while playing an up-pick.

Old-time Fiddle Tune

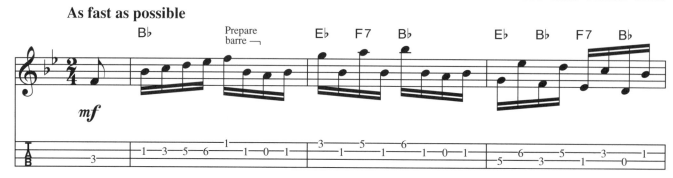

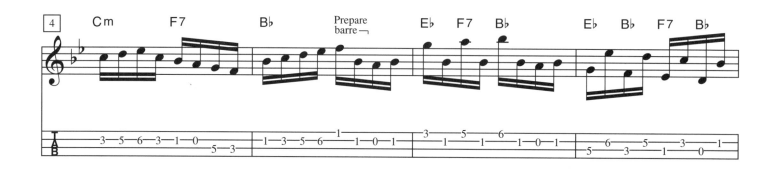

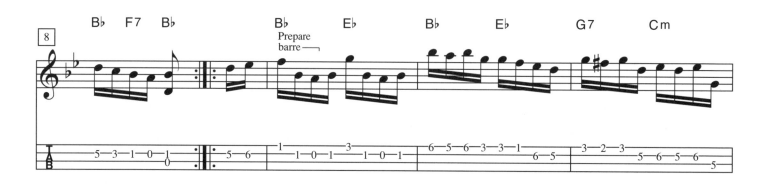

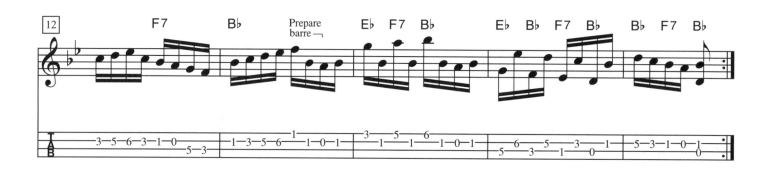

Special note to guitarists:
If you're accompanying this piece, place a capo across the 3rd fret and use the following chords:
For B♭ use G; for E♭ use C; for F7 use D7; for Cm use Am; for G7 use E7.

Li'l Liza Jane

Paying attention to details such as slides and articulations (staccato dots and tenuto dashes) will make this a terrific addition to your repertoire. In measure 2, the F♯ is held by keeping the 2nd finger down for the full two beats as the rest of the melody is played above.

American Folk Song

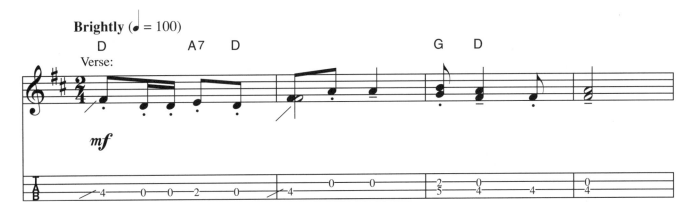

Verse:
I got a gal and you got none, Li'l Liza Jane,
I got a gal that calls me Hon, Li'l Liza Jane.

Chorus:
Oh, Eliza, L'il Liza Jane!
Oh, Eliza, Li'l Liza Jane!

Verse:
Gonna throw my cards away, Li'l Liza Jane
When you name the happy day, Li'l Liza Jane.
(repeat Chorus)

Little Maggie

This great mountain dance tune is based on a transposed Mixolydian mode (see note on "John Hardy").
The fills are based on the same mode, but the C natural is not used.

American Folk Song

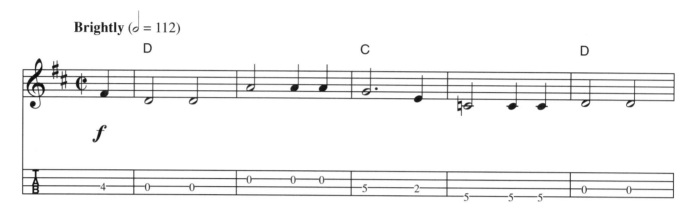

Well, yonder stands Little Maggie with a rum glass in her hand,
She's thinkin' 'bout her troubles while foolin' some other man.

Tell me, how can I ever stand it, just to see those two blue eyes,
They're shinin' like a diamond, like a diamond in the sky.

Now Maggie's goin' to the station with a suitcase in her hand,
She's goin' away for to leave me, she's goin' to some other man.

Old Joe Clark

The two-sharp key signature does not indicate the key of D major, but a transposed Mixolydian mode on A (A B C♯ D E F♯ G-natural). This is a popular mode for many country tunes (see "John Hardy" and "Little Maggie") and shows their ancient roots. The first section uses the open-string drone effect, but this time below the melody.

American Folk Song

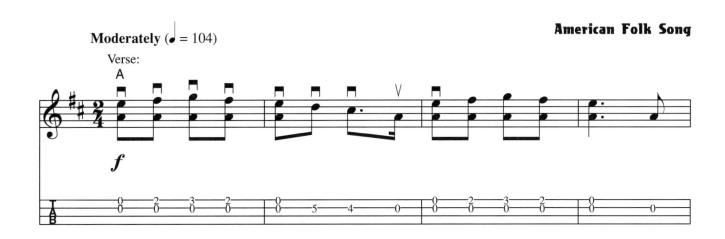

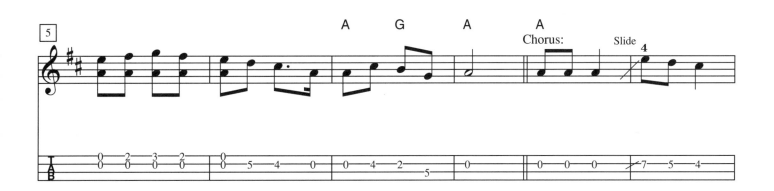

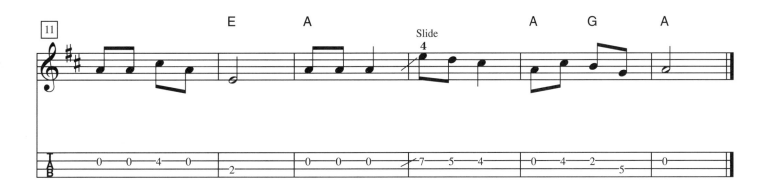

Verse:
I went up to old Joe's house,
Old Joe was not at home.
I eat up all his ham meat
And throwed away the bone.

Chorus:
Round and round, Old Joe Clark,
Round and round I say.
Round and round, Old Joe Clark,
I ain't got long to stay.

The Crawdad Song

This arrangement includes several fills (runs of notes that fill in spots in the melody where there are long-held notes or rests). In bluegrass, these are often based on a pentatonic (five-tone) scale. In this key, the pentatonic scale consists of the notes D, E, F♯, A, and B. You can use these notes to create your own fills. The arrangement also uses slides. In measure 11, for example, start a few frets below the written note; pick the string and slide up to the desired note, in this case, F-natural.

American Folk Song

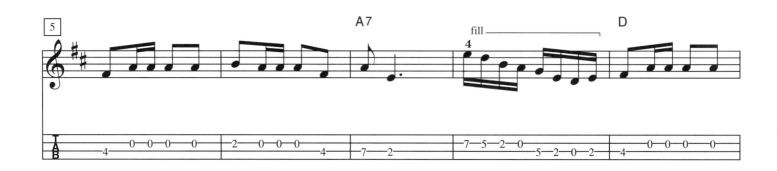

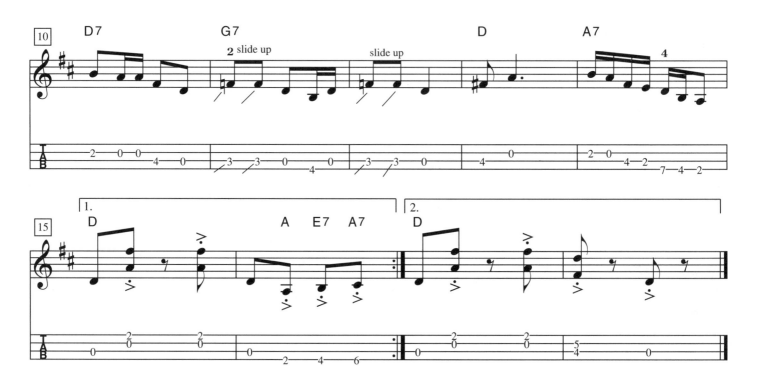

You get a line and I'll get a pole, honey,
You get a line and I'll get a pole, babe,
You get a line and I'll get a pole,
And we'll go down to the crawdad hole,
Honey, sugar baby mine.

Possum up a Gum Stump

This old fiddle tune features lots of fast picking and tricky fingering. Especially note the violent contrasts between loud and soft that occur from measure 9 to the end. The syncopations in measures 9, 11, and 13 are more than a little reminiscent of "Turkey in the Straw," but since the title appears in the lyric of the precursor to "Turkey," we know that "Possum" is the older tune.

Old-time Fiddle Tune

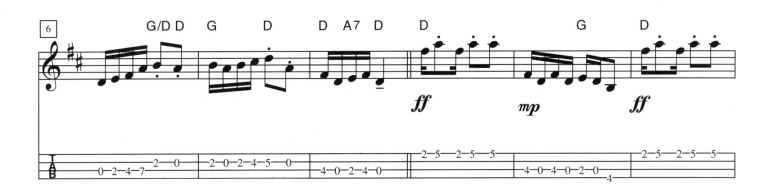

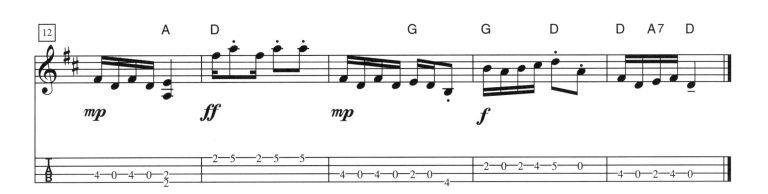

Possum up a gum stump, coney in the holler,
Little gal at my house, fat as she can waller.
Saddle up the ol' hoss, martingale and collar,
Fetch 'er down to my house, give you half a dollar.

Sally Goodin'

One of the most famous old-time fiddle tunes, it is adapted here for mandolin. The melody is usually played on the 2nd string below the open 1st string, which acts like the drone on a bagpipe or the unfingered 5th string of the five-string banjo. Use the 2nd finger to play the slides, which should start at least two frets below the C♯.

Old-time Fiddle Tune

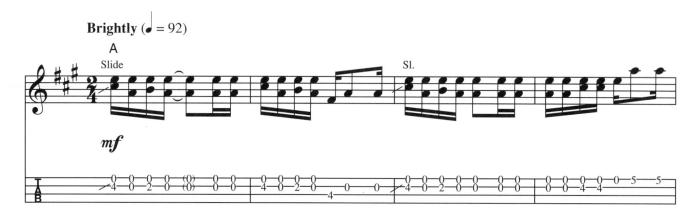

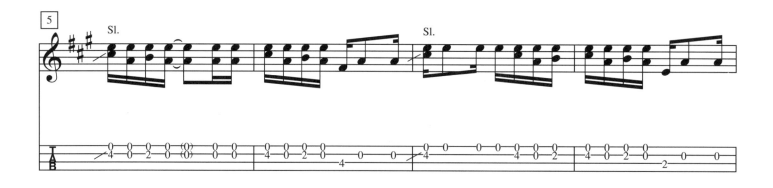

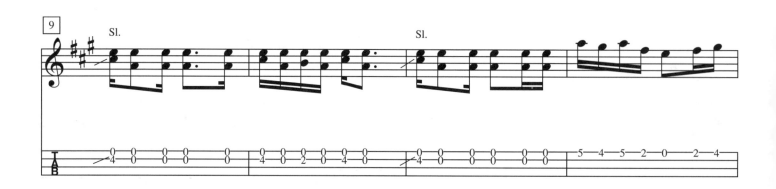

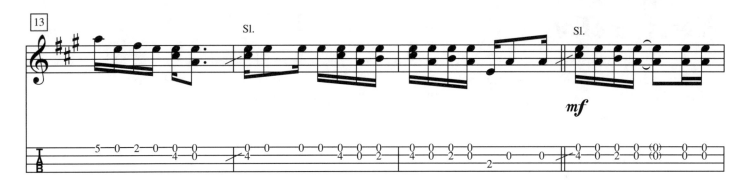

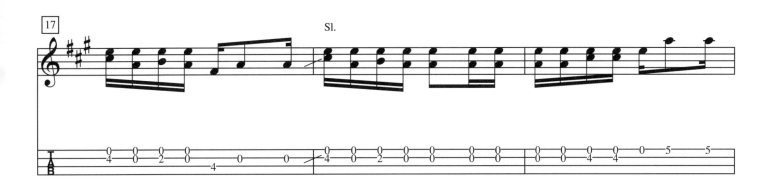

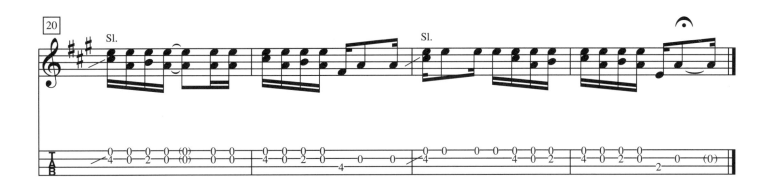

I had a piece o' pie, and I had a piece o' puddin',
And I gave it all away for to see Sally Goodin'.

A sheep and a cow a-walkin' in the pasture,
The sheep said, "Cow, can't you walk a little faster?"

I went to the river and the river was up,
Along came a coon and a yaller hound pup.

You had a piece o' pie and you had a piece o' puddin',
Now, don't you forget for to swing Sally Goodin'.

Pretty Polly

This marvelously atmospheric murder ballad is based on a six-note minor scale called a hexachord: D E F G A C. The arrangement takes advantage of the fact that the note D can be played either on the open string or on the 4th string, 7th fret. The melody is always accented. Play the fill-in chords a little softer. Follow the tablature carefully and this tune can become one of the high spots of your repertoire.

American Folk Song

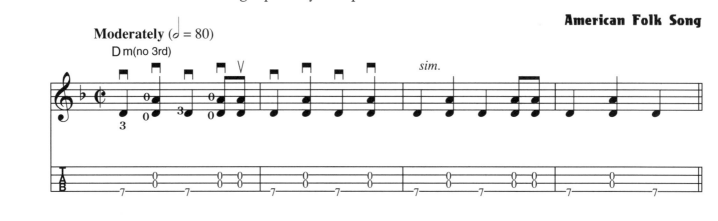

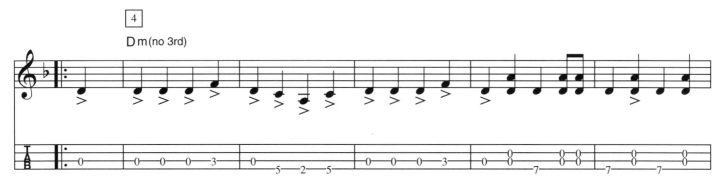

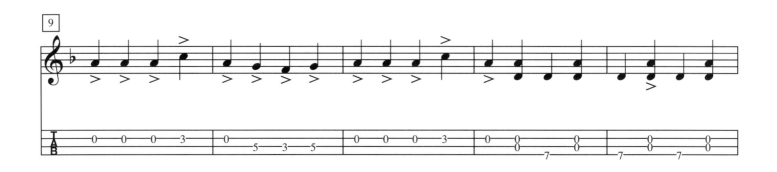

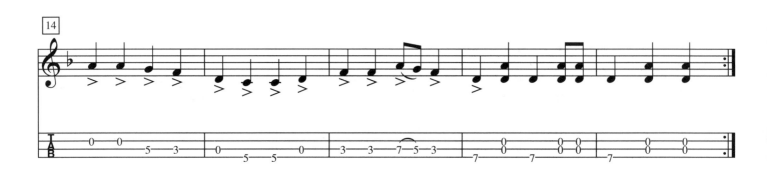

I used to be a rambler and I strayed from town to town;
I used to be a rambler and I strayed from town to town;
I courted Pretty Polly and her beauty's never been found.

I courted Pretty Polly the livelong night;
I courted Pretty Polly the livelong night;
Then left her next morning before it was light.

Skip to My Lou

With its many repeated notes, this famous square dance tune is a natural for the mandolin.
Use picking similar to that in the first two measures throughout.

Traditional Square Dance Tune

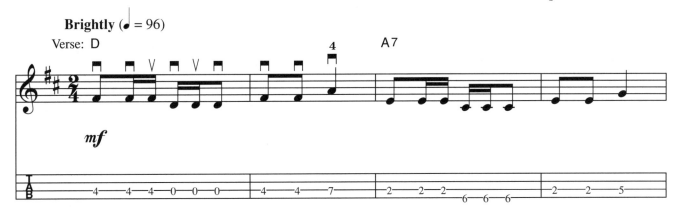

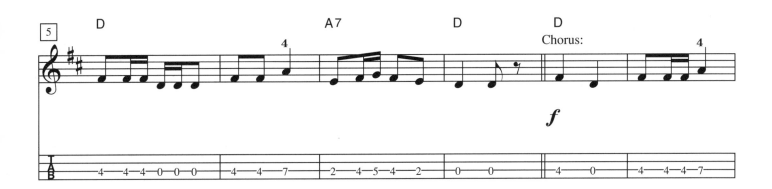

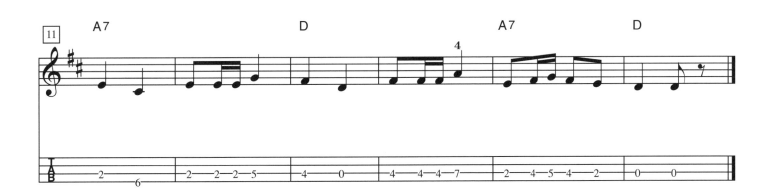

Verse:
Fly in the buttermilk, shoo, fly, shoo!
Fly in the buttermilk, shoo, fly, shoo!
Fly in the buttermilk, shoo, fly, shoo!
Skip to my Lou, my darlin'.

Chorus:
Skip, skip, skip to my Lou,
Skip, skip, skip to my Lou,
Skip, skip, skip to my Lou,
Skip to my Lou, my darlin'.

Soldier's Joy

This old-time fiddle tune makes a wonderful exercise for speed and dexterity. All eighth notes are played with downpicks. Play the 16ths with strict alternate picking. Since this arrangement goes above the first position, a certain amount of work is required to get the fingering down pat, but it's worth it.

Old-time Fiddle Tune

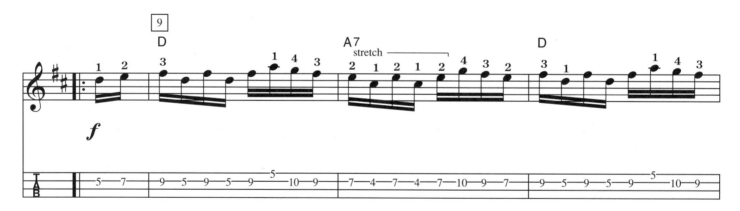

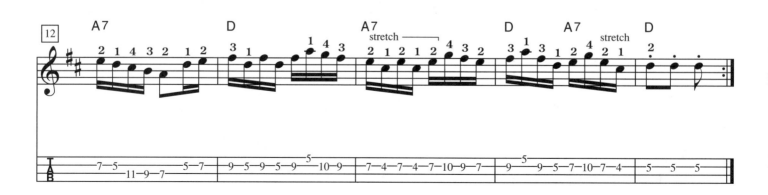

Turkey in the Straw

This famous song dates from the earliest days of minstrelsy and was first published with different words in 1835. The syncopations that appear in measures 7, 15, and many times in the chorus are an early example of African influence on American music. Years later, syncopation became an important element of ragtime and jazz.

Minstrel Song

Whoa, Mule, Whoa!

This arrangement uses a wonderful effect that no player of a single-note instrument can execute. The chorus places the melody below the harmony. Because the harmony doesn't move and the melody does, the melody will always stand out, even if you don't play it any louder.

American Folk Song

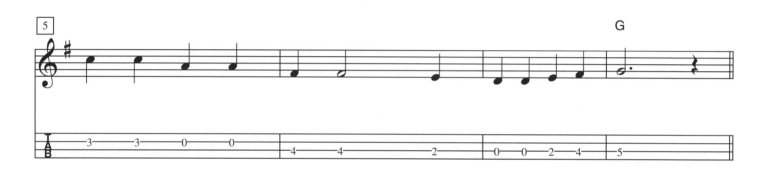

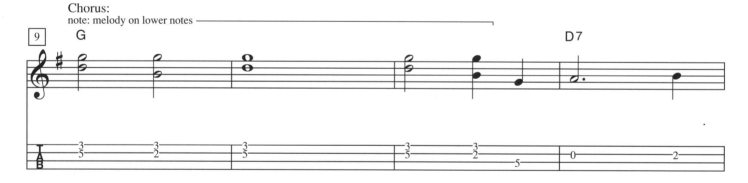

Verse:
I went to see Miss Liza,
She was standin' in the door.
Shoes and stockin's in her hand,
And feet all over the floor.

Chorus:
Whoa, mule, whoa!
Whoa, mule, I say!
Jus' hop right in, Miss Liza,
And hold on to the sleigh.

Wildwood Flower

This song came to be associated with the Carter Family due to their wonderful recording of it in the 1920s. The melody is constructed using the C major hexachord (six-note scale): C D E F G A. This strongly suggests that it has an ancient origin.

Country Song

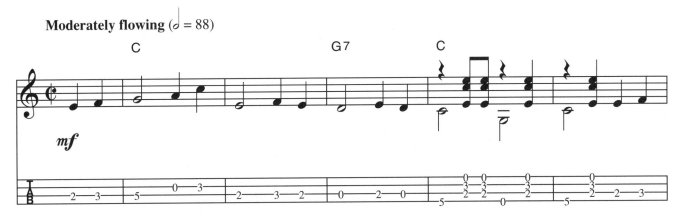

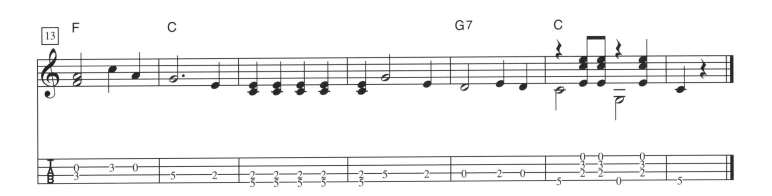

I'll entwine and I'll mingle my raven black hair,
With the roses so red and the lilies so fair.
Oh, the myrtle so bright with its emerald hue,
And a pale wildwood flower with petals so blue.

Chicken Reel

The first note, E♯ is identical with F natural. It is written as E♯ because it resolves upward to the F♯ that comes next. Pick the E♯ on the 1st string, 1st fret; keep firm pressure on the string and slide to the F♯ on the 2nd fret. If you do it right the F♯ will sound clearly, and you'll hear a musical version of a chicken's cackle.

American Dance Tune

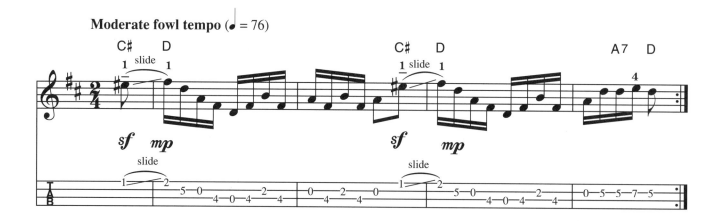

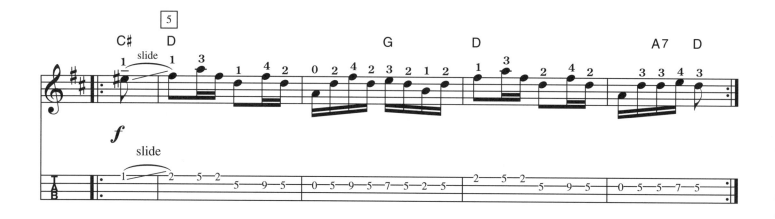

Delaware Hornpipe

Some authorities assert that a hornpipe was a folk dance dedicated to an obscure figure named Herne, the Hunter. Others claim it is a sailor's dance that pantomimes "weigh anchor," "haul in the sails," and other aspects of the sailor's life. All eighth notes get downpicks. Use strict alternating down-and-up strokes on the 16th notes. This technique is called *crosspicking* and a lot of practice is needed to get it up to speed.

Traditional Fiddle Tune

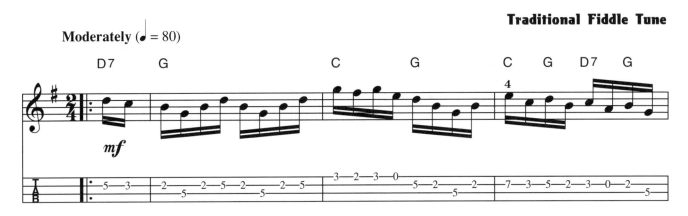

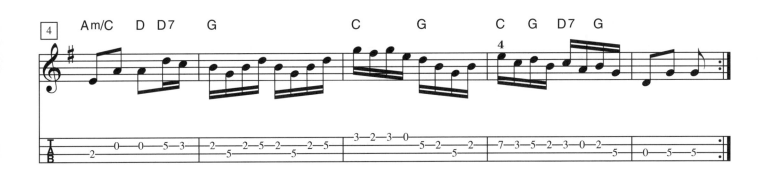

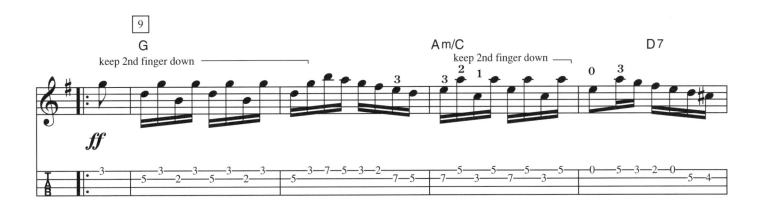

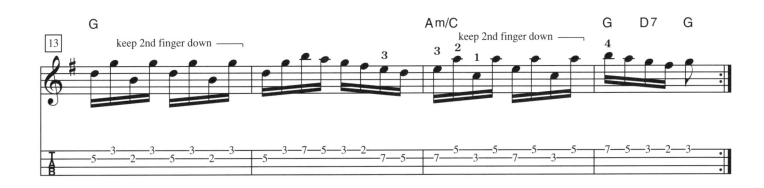

Sailor's Hornpipe

Fans of old Popeye cartoons will recognize this one. Because there were no women on the old sailing ships, sailors made up dances they could either do alone or with each other. Hornpipes imitated the motions sailors made when performing their ordinary tasks. Because of the cramped conditions on ships, hornpipes were designed to be danced in a very limited space. (Also see notes on "The Drunken Sailor.")

Sailor's Dance

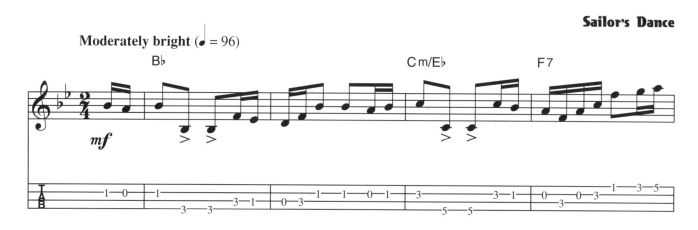

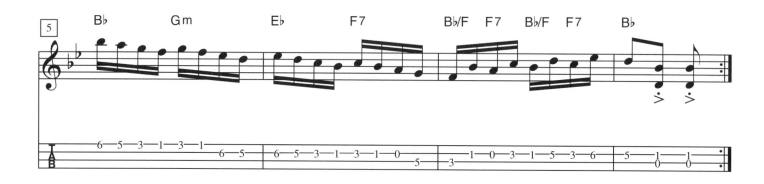

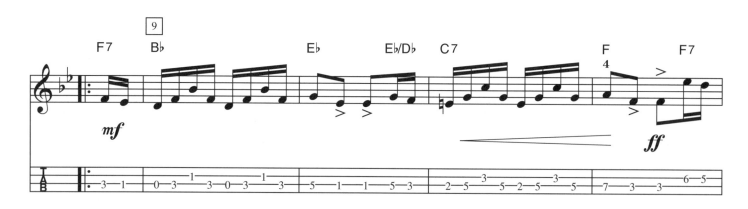

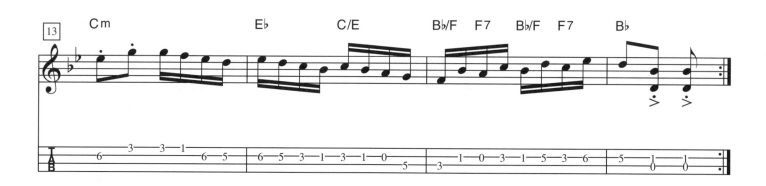

The White Cockade

You may not recognize the title, but the tune will probably be familiar. Follow the fingering and articulations (expression marks) carefully. Notes with a staccato dot, such as the first B in meas. 2, are cut off short. Notes with a tenuto dash, such as the 2nd B in meas. 2, are held out to their full value and slightly accented. Paying attention to details like these will give your playing a professional polish.

Virginia Reel

Ah! Marie

This arrangement of one of the most popular Italian songs ever written follows the original fairly closely. The technique used in measures 1, 2, 10 and elsewhere is called a broken chord. To play it effectively, finger the complete chord and then pick the proper notes.

Andantino (not too fast and somewhat freely)

Eduardo di Capua

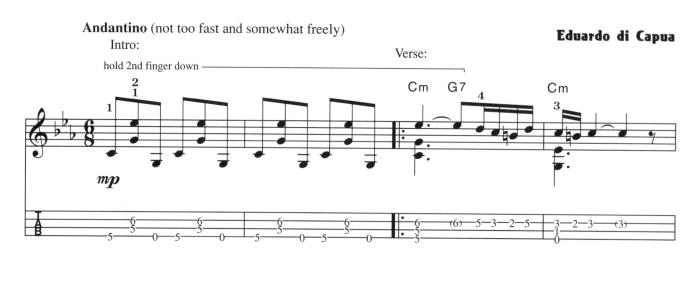

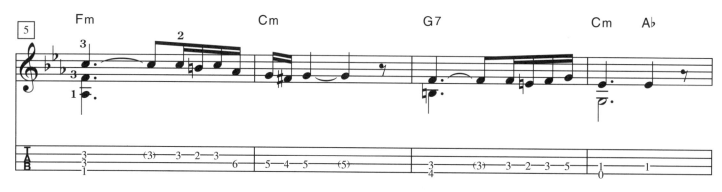

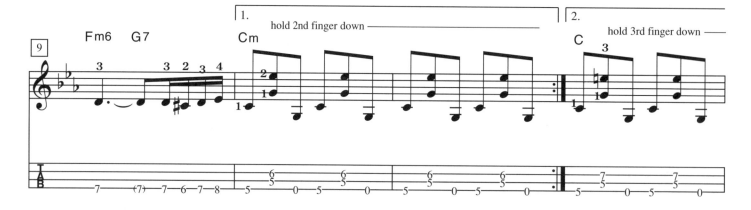

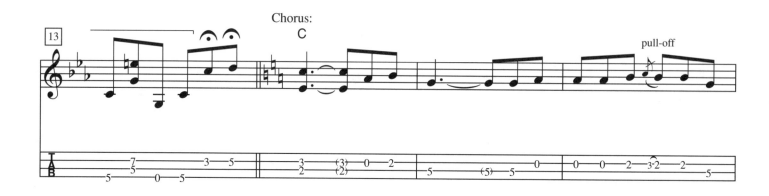

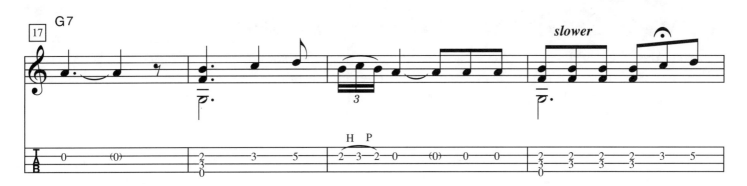

Verse:
Arapete, fenesta,
Famm'affaccia Maria,
Castongo mmiez"avia,
Speruto p"a vede.
Nun trovo n'ora'e pace;
'A nott"a faccio juorno,
Sempe pe stacca_atuorno,
Speranno'e ce parla.

Chorus:
Ah! Maria, Marie!
Quanta suonno che perdo pe te;
Famm'addurmi,
Abbracciato un poco cu te!
Ah! Maria, Marie!
Quanta suonno che perdo pe te;
Famm'addurmi,
Oj, Mari!
Oj, Mari!

Torna a Surriento (Come Back to Sorrento)

Certainly, this is one of the most famous Italian songs ever written. Sorrento is a resort town about an hour south of Naples, across the bay from the Isle of Capri. There's even a statue of the composer on Sorrento's main street. Use plenty of tremolo and maintain a flexible sense of time on this Italian classic.

Ernesto de Curtis

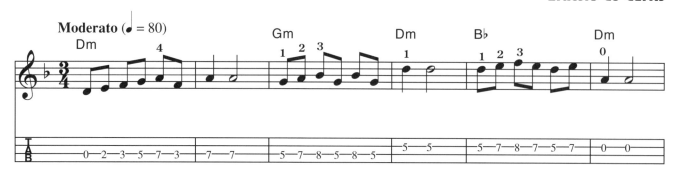

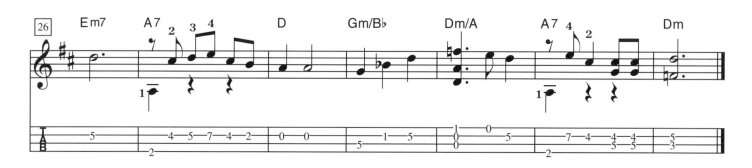

Roman Guitar (Chitarra Romana)

Although the tango originally developed in the slums of Buenos Aires in the 1880s, the dance soon became popular throughout the world. This 1936 composition is a fine example of an Italian tango, and it has become a standard. Play the interludes short and crisp. The verse and chorus are legato, so use a lot of tremolo. All triplets and double grace-notes are played as hammer-ons and pull-offs. Pay close attention to the fingering, which will allow you to play this arrangement four beats to each measure at the proper speed of 120 beats-per-minute.

English Lyric by Marjorie Harper
Music by E. di Lazzaro

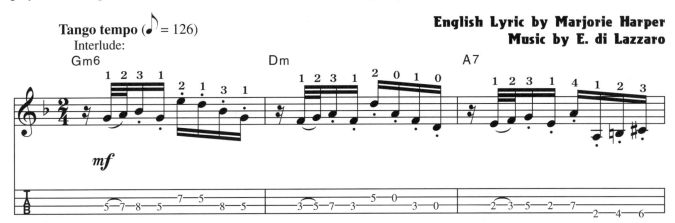

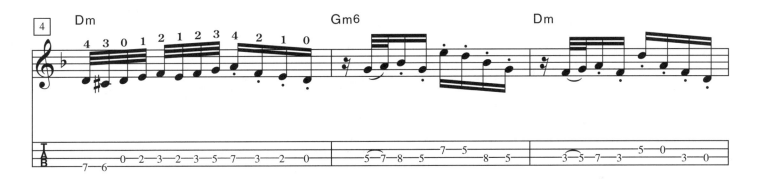

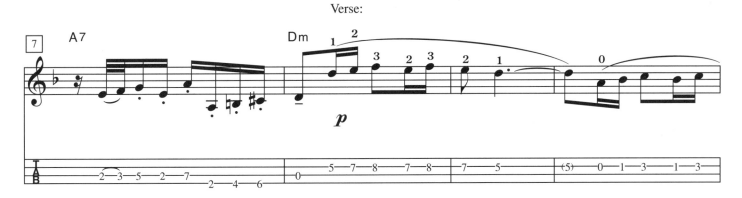

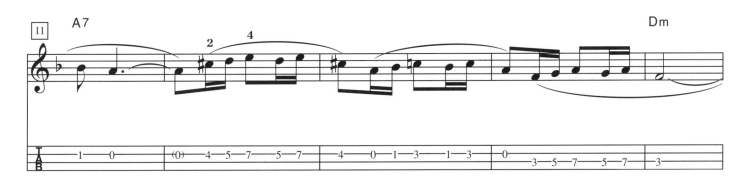

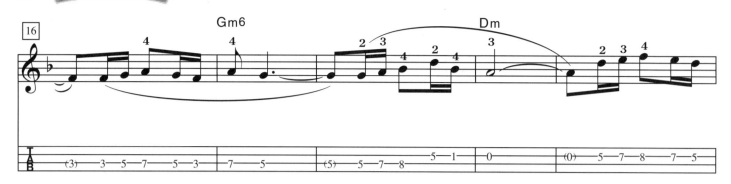

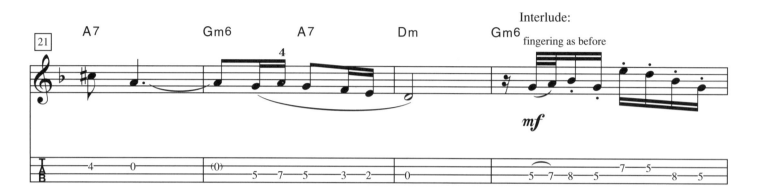

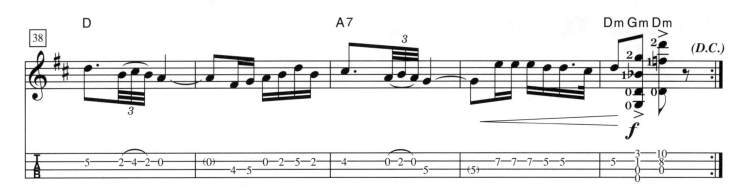

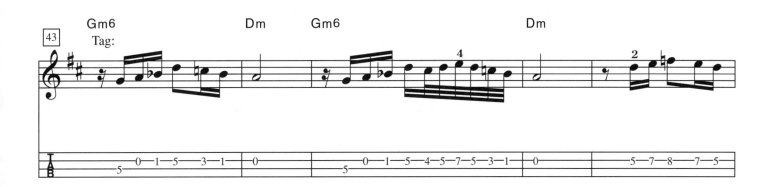

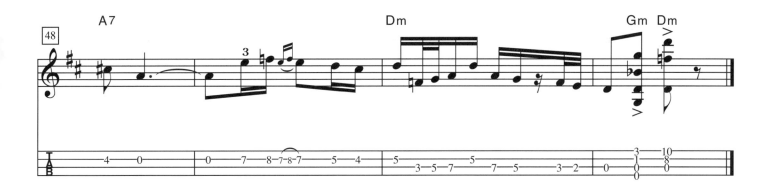

Verse:
Purple shadows are creeping,
And the fountain is weeping;
Hear the trees gently sigh,
While the winds murmur by,
As they ride from afar.

All my mem'ries awaken,
'Neath each bright watching star;
Play for one who's forsaken,
Oh, my Roman guitar!

Chorus:
Now I'm singing in the shadows,
My guitar is all that's left for me;
Let it comfort me with melody,
O, console me, my guitar!

Now my heart is in the shadows,
For there's no one on her balcony,
And I'm singing to a memory,
Whisper softly, my guitar!

Tag:
Play to me in the shadows,
Oh, my Roman guitar!

Wedding Tarantella

It's virtually impossible to go to any Italian affair without hearing this famous tune. The tarantella is a wild dance once thought to counteract insanity brought on by the bite of the tarantula. Actually, despite the spider's fearsome appearance, the tarantula's bite is harmless.

Sicilian Folk Dance

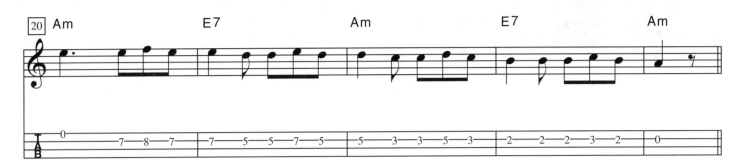

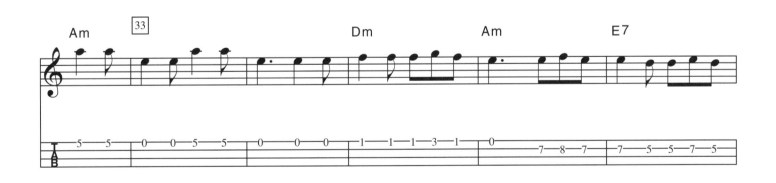

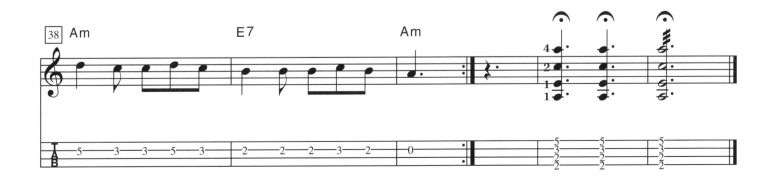

O Sole Mio!

No, the name of this piece is not "O Solo Mio." The correct title means "Oh, my sun." The Three Tenors always got ecstatic cheers when they sang this famous Italian song, and as "It's Now Or Never," the song was a hit for Elvis Presley. Use lots of tremolo throughout and play the melody as legato (smoothly and joined) as possible.

Eduardo di Capua

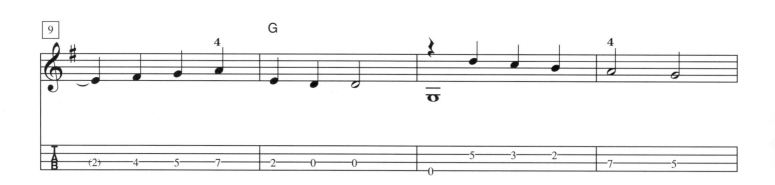

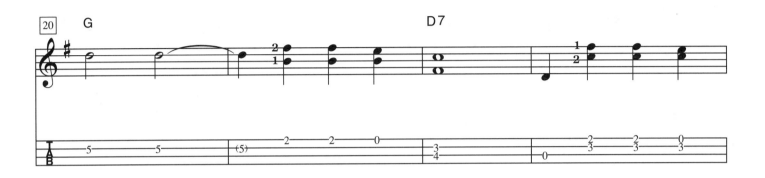

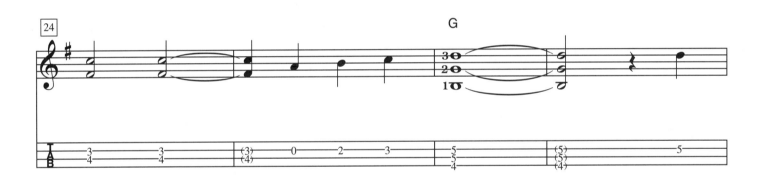

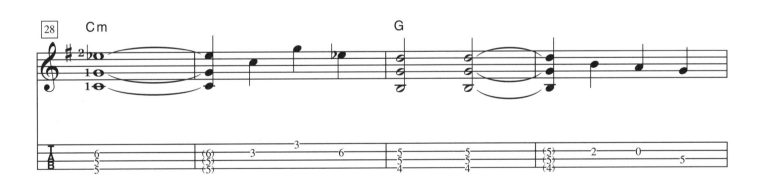

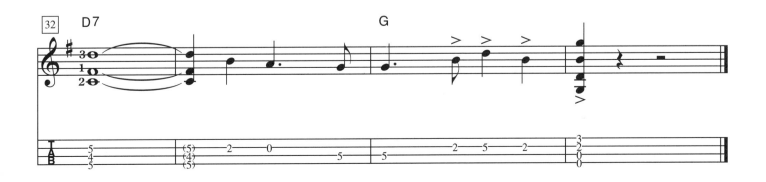

Funiculi–Funicula

This lively song is as popular today as when it was written over a hundred years ago. Who can resist banging on the table to its lively chorus? Use plenty of tremolo on the longer notes. When using tremolo on a chord (e.g. measure 5) strike the whole chord with a downpick and then tremolo on the highest note only. Using tremolo across the entire chord tends to sound sloppy, creating so much string noise that the beauty of the melody is spoiled.

Luigi Denza

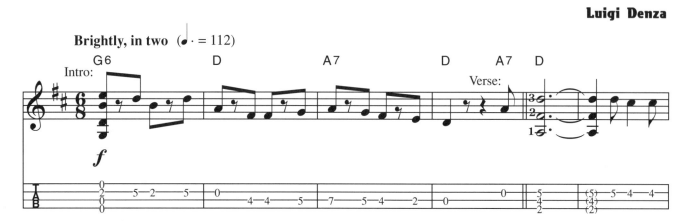

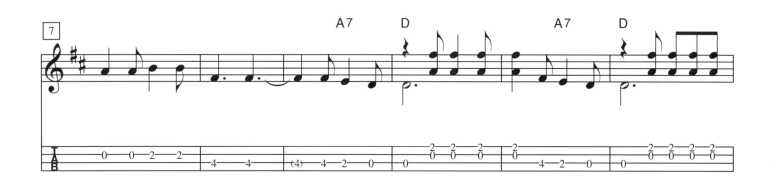

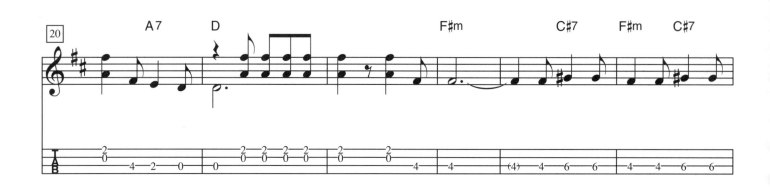

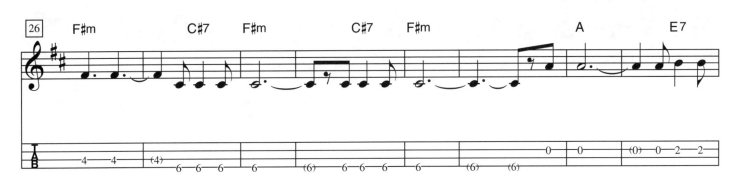

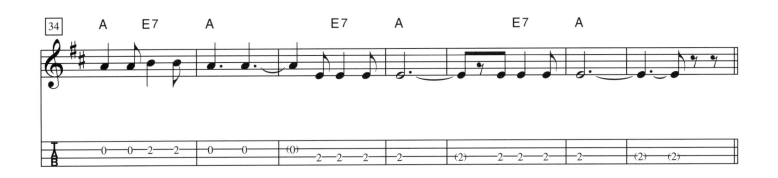

Chorus:

note: melody below harmony

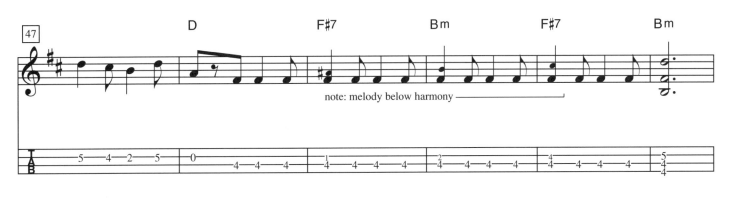

Ah! Vous Dirai-Je, Maman (Twinkle, Twinkle, Little Star)

The title means "How I Would Like to Tell You, Mother," and is a song of loving appreciation from a child. The melody must have been well known as early as the 18th century, as it was the basis of a series of variations by Mozart. In English-speaking countries it became known as "Twinkle, Twinkle, Little Star," "Baa, Baa, Black Sheep," and "The Alphabet Song." Whatever the title, it's one of the most famous melodies ever written and is instantly recognizable to every child.

French Folk Song

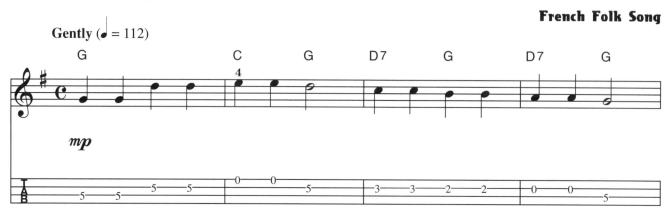

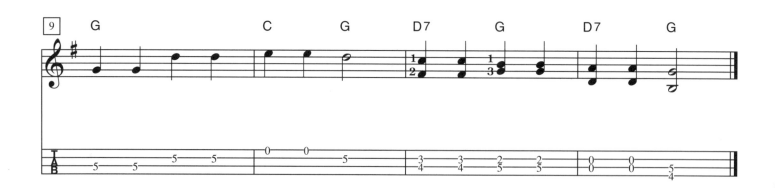

Traditional French Lyric:
Ah! vous dirai-je, maman
Qui j' a-dore a tout moment.
Heureux destin qui me donne
Une mere tendre et bonne,
Et si bonne' que chacque enfant
Voudrait l' avoir pour maman.

Traditional English Lyric:
Twinkle, twinkle, little star,
How I wonder what you are.
Up above the world so high,
Like a diamond in the sky,
Twinkle, twinkle, little star,
How I wonder what you are.

All Through the Night

This arrangement contrasts several different techniques. Measures 1 and 2 present the melody in single notes, almost like a solo singer. Then measures 3 and 4 answer with two-note chords, like a choral answer. Measures 9, 10, and 11 use the open D string as a pedal point between the melody notes.

Welsh Folk Song

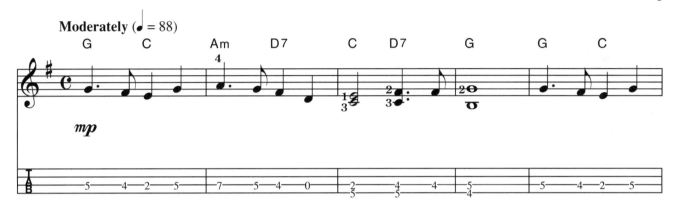

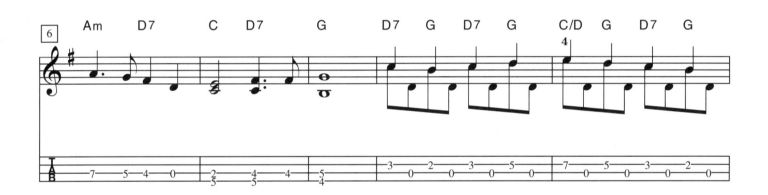

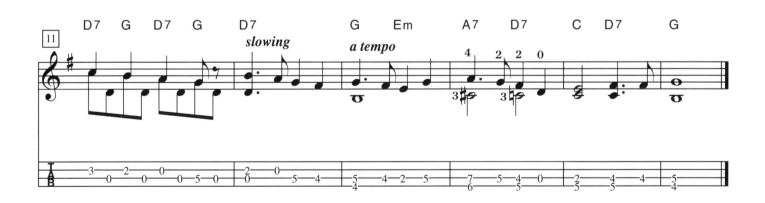

Sleep, my child, and peace attend thee all through the night.
Guardian angels God will send thee all through the night.
Soft the drowsy hours are creeping
Hill and vale in slumber sleeping,
I, my loving vigil keeping, all through the night.

The Ash Grove

When playing this lovely, simple English folk song, concentrate on producing a clear, silvery tone, and pay attention to all staccato marks. In Great Britain the ash tree was thought to have magical powers, including the curing of warts and diseased farm animals. The sap from the ash was used to ward off witches' charms and protect against venomous snakes.

English Folk Song

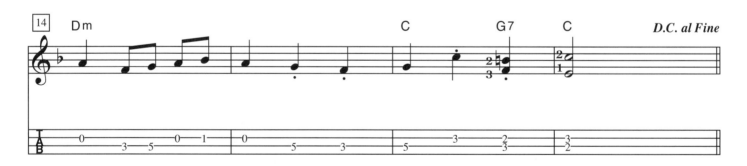

Down yonder green valley where streamlets meander,
When twilight is fading, I pensively roam.
Or at the bright noontide in solitude wander,
Amid the dark shades of the lonely ash grove.
'Twas there while the blackbird was cheerfully singing,
I first met that dear one, the joy of my heart.
Around as for gladness the bluebells were ringing,
Ah! then little thought I how soon we should part.

The Flower of Monemvasy

This dance, in typical Greek 7/8 meter, is played as one measure of 3/8 followed by a measure of 2/4. Keep the eighth notes even and don't allow the 3/8 measures to turn into triplets. The scale used for this composition is rather exotic. Although the piece is in A, it uses a two-flat key signature. The six-note scale uses the notes A B♭ C♯ D E♭ G.

Greek Dance

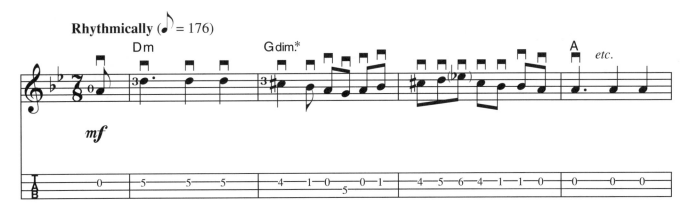

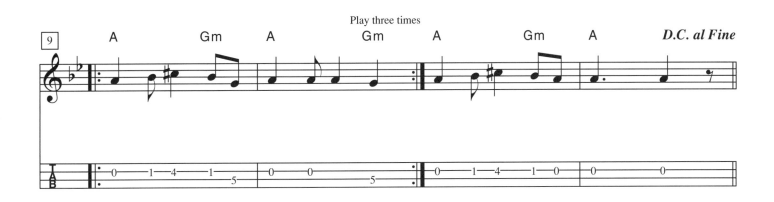

* In accompanying this song make sure to use Gdim(no E) in these two places.
Diagrams for this chord can be found for guitar on page 148 and for mandolin on page 149.

For He's a Jolly Good Fellow

This tune has become famous with at least four different sets of words. Its first version was an 18th-century tune called "Malbrouk" which was about the Duke of Marlboro's military victories in the early 1700s. During the reign of the ill-fated French king Louis XVI, it was known as a lullaby. By the 1840s it had surfaced in America as "We Won't Go Home Till Morning." In 1870 there was a printed version called "For He's a Jolly Good Fellow," almost certainly of British origin—Americans don't usually say "jolly." Its most recent form is "The Bear Went Over the Mountain," which is certainly American—there are no bears in England.

Words: Anonymous
Music: French Folk Song

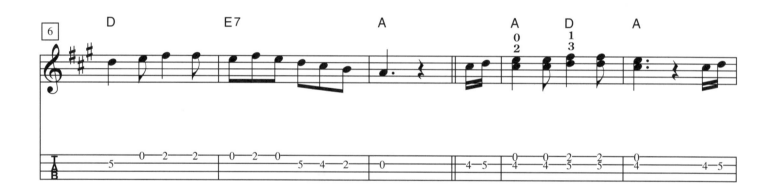

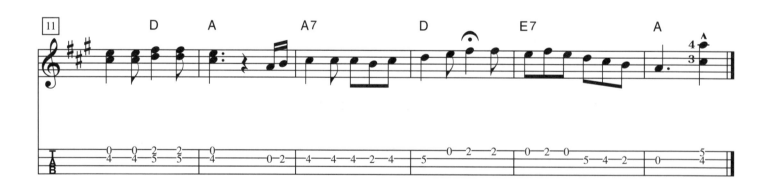

(based on first eight measures)

For he's a jolly good fellow, (3 times)
And so say all of we.

And so say all of we, (2 times)
For he's a jolly good fellow,
And so say all of we.

The bear went over the mountain, (3 times)
And whaddya think he saw?

He saw another mountain, (3 times)
And whaddya think he did?

Podmoskovnye Vyechera (Midnight in Moscow)

This Russian song, composed in folk style, has become a great favorite in the Jewish culture. As "Midnight in Moscow," it also became a hit recording in Dixieland-jazz style. For an authentic Russian sound, use a lot of tremolo and play the first eight measures slowly. Then, starting at measure nine, gradually increase the tempo until you're playing it as fast as possible. You can stretch out this effect over several repetitions.

Matosovsky/Soloviev-Sedoy

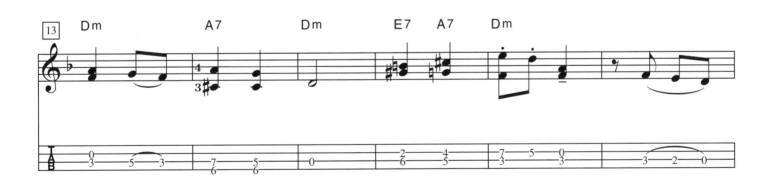

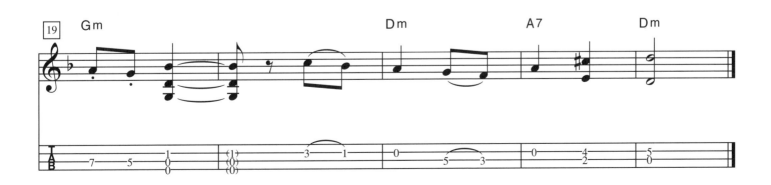

Two Guitars

This famous Gypsy melody is a natural for the mandolin. The first 24 measures actually have two different planes of action; an artistic player will use contrasting dynamics to keep them separate, i.e., playing the lower notes softer than the higher ones. The final section goes rather high, but the tablature will tell you where to find these notes.

Russian Gypsy Melody

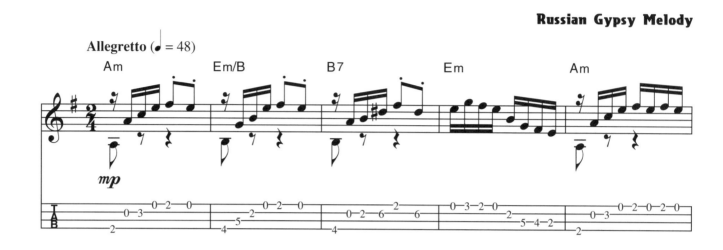

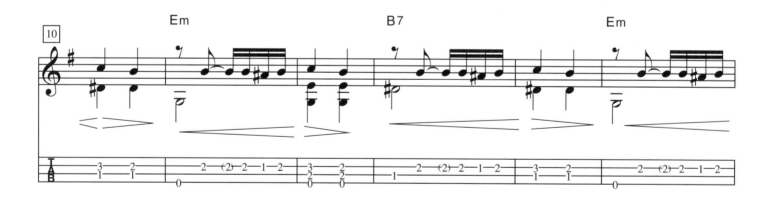

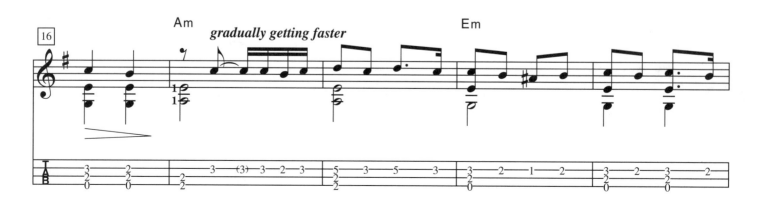

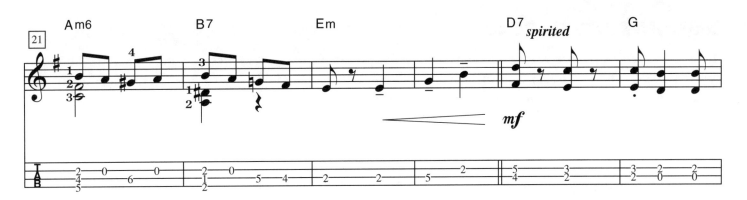

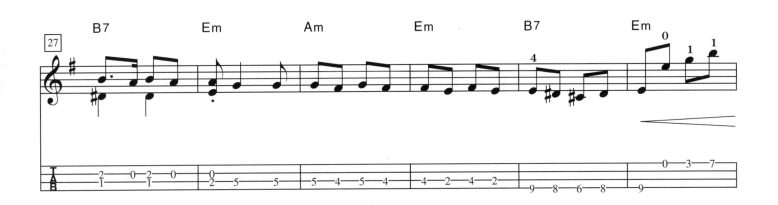

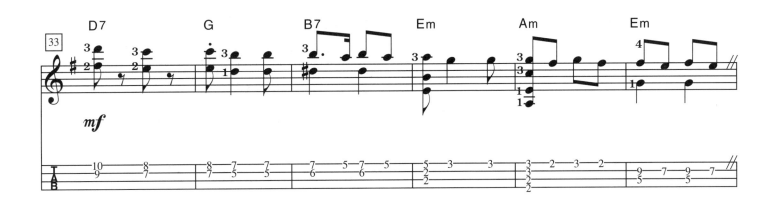

Scarborough Fair

This lovely song dates back at least 400 years. In the 1960s it was given a very successful modern treatment by the folk duo Simon and Garfunkel. The melody is based on the Dorian mode (D E F G A B C), in this arrangement transposed up a whole tone to make it more suitable for the mandolin.

English Folk Song

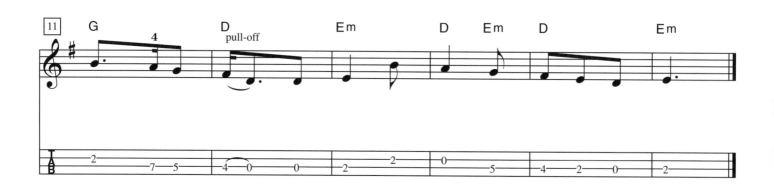

Are you goin' to Scarborough Fair?
Parsley, sage, rosemary and thyme.
Remember me to one who lives there,
For she once was a true love of mine.

Have her make me a fine cambric shirt,
Parsley, sage, rosemary and thyme.
Without no seam or rough needlework,
And she will be a true love of mine.

Amazing Grace

Sea captain John Newton wrote these powerful words after a terrible storm almost sank the slave ship he was piloting. He gave up his evil trade and became a minister and composer of hymns. The arrangement is not difficult, so concentrate on tone and the clean execution of the pull-offs. Tremolo only on the longer notes.

Words by John Newton
Music: Anonymous

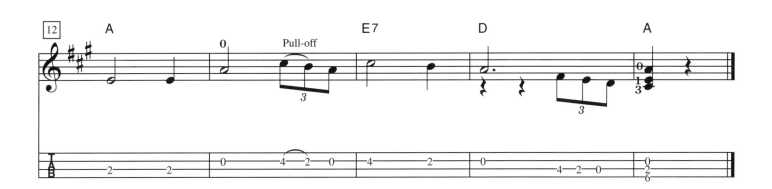

Amazing grace, how sweet the sound that saved a wretch like me!
I once was lost, but now am found, was blind but now I see.

Through many dangers, toils, and snares I have already come.
'Tis grace has brought me safe thus far, and grace will lead me home.

I've Got Peace Like a River

Play this great old gospel tune with a full tone and little, if any, tremolo. To get a clear, rich sound on the chords, follow the fingering and practice slowly.

African–American Gospel Song

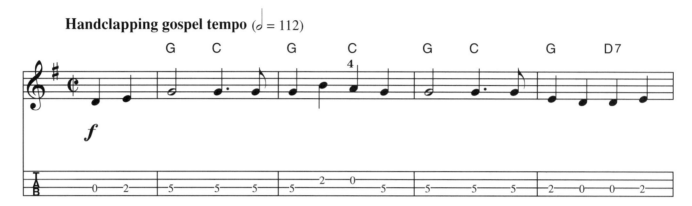

I've got peace like a river,
I've got peace like a river,
I've got peace like a river in my soul.

I've got peace like a river,
I've got peace like a river,
I've got peace like a river in my soul.

Simple Gifts ('Tis the Gift to be Simple)

The Shakers were a religious sect who founded several settlements in the northeast United States during the early 19th century. This song expresses their philosophy of simplicity, humility, and austere beauty which also inspired their furniture design and architecture that are so prized today.

Joseph Brackett

'Tis the gift to be simple,'tis the gift to be free.
'Tis the gift to come down where we ought to be,
And when we find ourselves in the place just right,
'Twill be in the valley of love and delight.

When true simplicity is gained,
To bow and to bend we shan't be ashamed.
To turn, turn, will be our delight,
Till by turning, turning we come out right.

Aura Lea

This song achieved great popularity with both sides during the American Civil War. In 1865, a version with new words called "Army Blue" was sung as the West Point graduation song. Its most recent incarnation was as "Love Me Tender," which Elvis Presley sang in a movie about the War Between the States. The notes are not very hard to play, so concentrate on getting a pure, silvery tone. Note the spelling of "Lea," often misspelled "Lee."

Words by W. W. Fosdick
Music by George R. Poulton

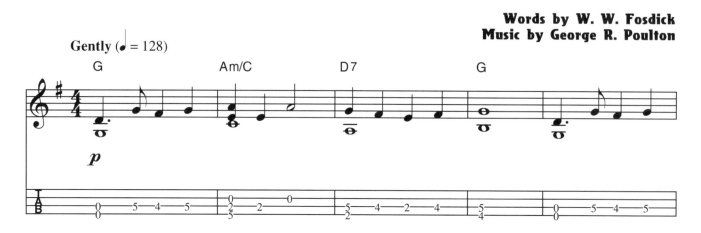

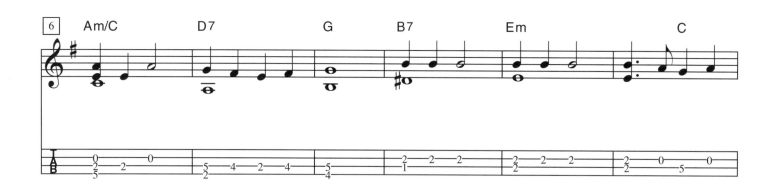

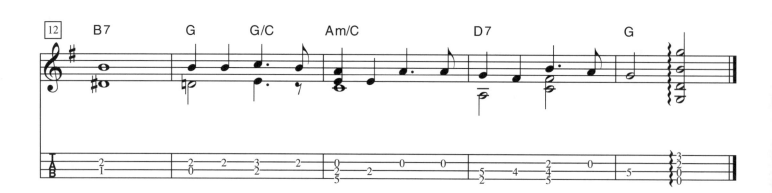

When the blackbird in the spring on the willow tree,
Sat and rocked, I heard him sing, singing "Aura Lea."
Aura Lea, Aura Lea, maid of golden hair;
Sunshine came along with thee, and swallows in the air.

Buffalo Gals

Early vaudevillians used to sing this song and insert the name of the town in which they were performing, "Chicago gals...," "New York gals...," etc. For some reason only Buffalo gals survived. Notice the syncopated figures in measures 7, 9, 10, etc., which are typical of early African-influenced songs (see "Turkey in the Straw," "Coney in the Creek," and many others).

American Folk Song

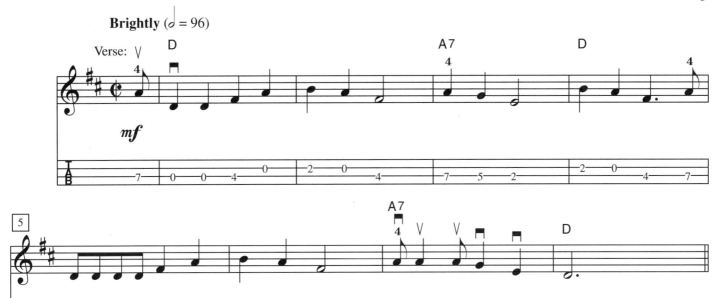

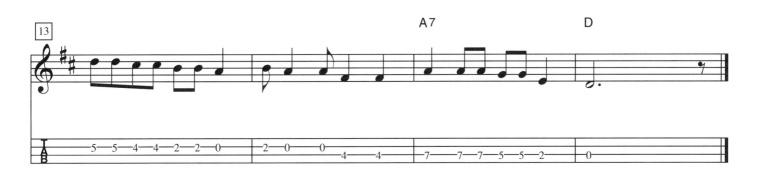

Verse:
As I was walking down the street,
Down the street, down the street.
A pretty little girl I chanced to meet,
Under the silvery moon.

Chorus:
Buffalo gals, wontcha come out tonight,
Come out tonight, come out tonight.
Buffalo gals wontcha come out tonight,
And dance by the light of the moon.

Golden Slippers

Written in 1879 by one of the first, if not the first, published African-American songwriters, its original title was "Oh! Dem Golden Slippers." Like many of the songs written for the minstrel stage, it contained a lot of dialect that today we would find offensive. Notice the fingering on the opening strain. By playing the melody entirely on the 2nd string a lot of awkward fingering and crosspicking is avoided.

Words and Music by
James A. Bland

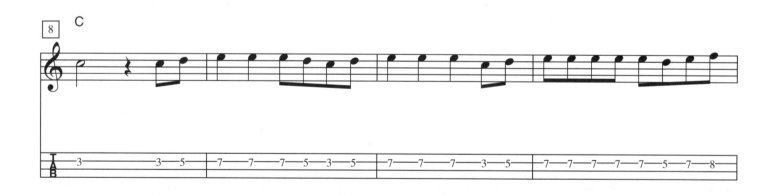

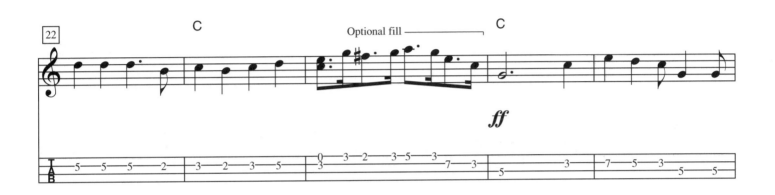

Verse:
Oh, my golden slippers are laid away,
'Cause I don't expect to wear 'em till my weddin' day.
And my long-tailed coat that I loved so well,
I will wear up in the chariot in the morn.
And my long white robe that I bought last June,
I'm a-gonna get changed cause it fits too soon.
And the old gray hoss that I used to drive,
I will hitch him to the chariot in the morn.

Chorus:
Oh, them golden slippers!
Oh, them golden slippers!
Golden slippers I'm a-gonna wear,
Because they look so neat.
Oh, them golden slippers!
Oh, them golden slippers!
Golden slippers I'm a-gonna wear,
To walk the golden street.

Camptown Races

Stephen Foster was probably the best American songwriter of the 1800s. Although he wrote many songs that were popular then—and quite a few that still are—he died broke and alone at the age of only 38. Especially of interest in this arrangement is measure eight, which requires a fast slide of the 2nd finger. The syncopation in measure 23 shows the influence that African music had on Foster's songs.

Stephen Foster

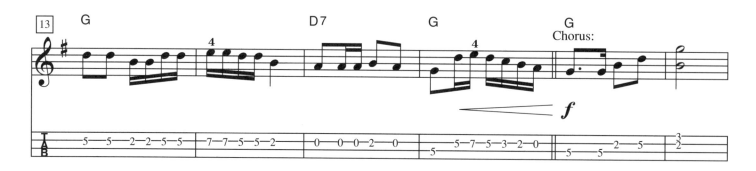

Verse:
Camptown ladies sing this song,
Doodah! Doodah!
Camptown racetrack's five miles long,
Oh! doodah day.

I came down there with my hat
 caved in, Doodah! Doodah!
Goin' back home with a pocket
 full o' tin,
Oh! doodah day!

Chorus:
Goin' to run all night,
Goin' to run all day.
I bet my money on a bobtail nag,
Somebody bet on the bay.

Good Night, Ladies

At old-time dances this song was always played as the last tune of the evening. Its origins are in minstrelsy; a similar song was composed and sung by minstrel-man E. P. Christy in 1847. The melody of the first eight measures is an embellishment of "Someone's in the Kitchen with Dinah." The last eight measures are a rewrite of "Mary Had a Little Lamb."

Minstrel Song

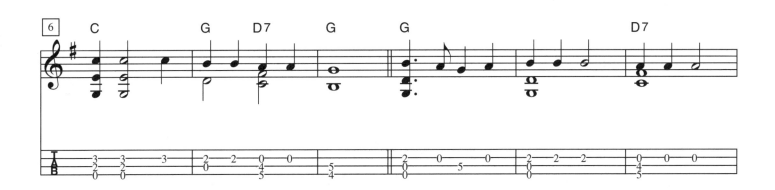

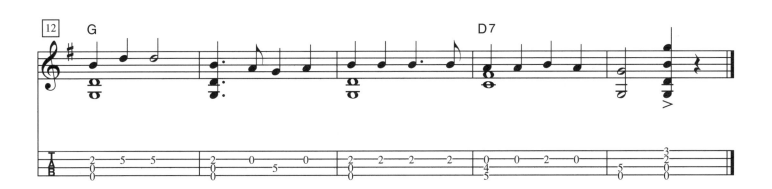

Good night, ladies! (3 times)
We're goin' to leave you now.

Merrily we roll along,
Roll along, roll along.
Merrily we roll along,
O'er the deep blue sea.

Listen to the Mockingbird

Here's something for all you fans of *The Three Stooges* (even if you won't admit it!). Their theme was written all the way back in 1855 by well-known songwriter Septimus Winner, who used a female pseudonym to appeal more strongly to the main audience for this type of sentimental ballad. The many repeated notes in the melody make it a natural for the mandolin.

by Alice Hawthorne
(Septimus Winner)

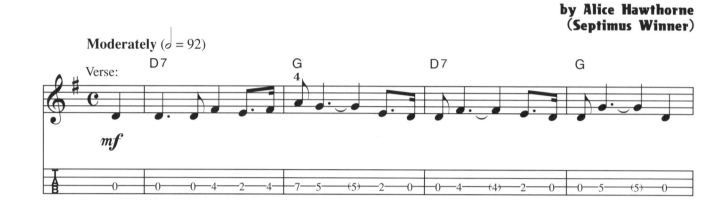

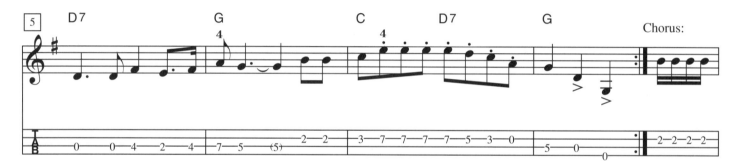

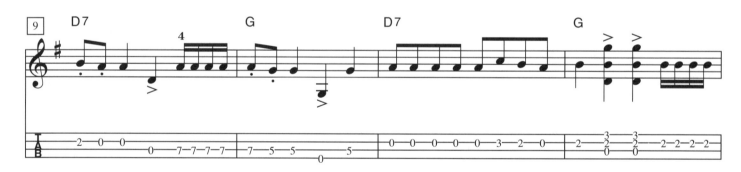

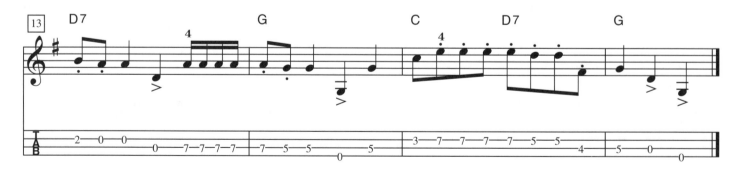

Verse:

I'm dreaming now of Hally, sweet Hally, sweet Hally;
I'm dreaming now of Hally,
For the thought of her is one that never dies.
She's sleeping in the valley, the valley, the valley;
She's sleeping in the valley,
And the mockingbird is singing where she lies.

Chorus:

Listen to the mockingbird, listen to the mockingbird,
The mockingbird still singing o'er her grave;
Listen to the mockingbird, listen to the mockingbird,
Still singing where the weeping willows wave.

Little Brown Jug

This tune has had many lives. It started out as a comic minstrel song, was given a famous swing treatment by the Glenn Miller Band in the 1940s and has also been recorded as a polka. This version sticks pretty close to the original vaudeville sound.

"Eastburn"
(Joseph E. Winner)

My wife and I lived all alone,
In a little log hut we called our own.
She loved gin and I loved rum,
I tell you we had lots of fun!

Ha! Ha! Ha! You and me,
Little brown jug how I love thee!
Ha! Ha! Ha! You and me,
Little brown jug how I love thee!

Ol' Dan Tucker

Written for the minstrel stage in 1843 by the man who composed "Dixie" 15 years later, this song should be played with a strong rhythmic feeling, somewhat like a banjo might play it. Start the opening triplet with an up-pick and you'll land on the downbeat with a downpick.

Dan D. Emmett

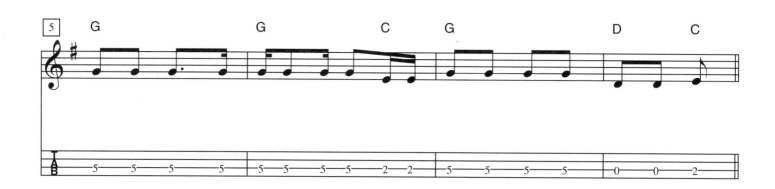

Verse:
I came to town the other night,
I heard the noise and saw the fight.
The watchman was a-runnin' around,
Cryin', "Ol' Dan Tucker's come to town!"

Chorus:
So get out the way, (instrumental)
Get out the way, (inst.)
Get out the way! Old Dan Tucker,
You're too late to come to supper.
(Interlude)

Verse:
Dan Tucker is a nice old man,
He used to ride our darby ram.
He sent him whizzin' down the hill;
If he hadn't got up he'd be there still!
(repeat Chorus and Interlude)

Verse:
Well, Ol' Dan Tucker an' I got drunk,
He fell in the fire an' kick up a chunk.
The charcoal got inside his shoe;
Lord, bless you, honey, how the ashes flew!
(repeat Chorus and Interlude)

The Old Gray Mare

First published in 1858 as "Down in Alabam'," this song was written by J. Warner for the Bryant Brothers, famous minstrel performers who used it in their grand finale, a part of the show called the "walkaround." It wasn't until many years later that an anonymous writer wrote this parody, which soon became better known than the original. Use swing eighth-notes for the proper feel in this arrangement. In the swing feel, downbeat eighth-notes are played slightly longer than upbeat eighths.

Words: Anonymous
Music by J. Warner

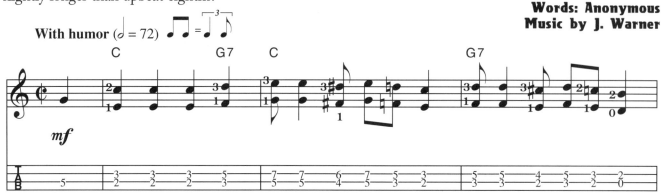

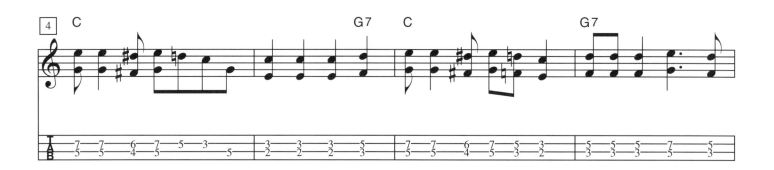

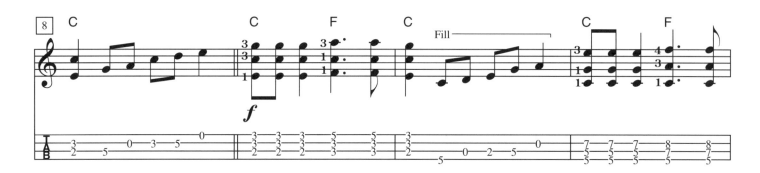

The old gray mare, she ain't what she used to be,
Ain't what she used to be, ain't what she used to be.
The old gray mare, she ain't what she used to be
Many long years ago.

Many long years ago, many long years ago.
The old gray mare, she ain't what she used to be
Many long years ago.

Reuben and Rachel

Also known as "Reuben, Reuben," this comic song, long a mainstay of the minstrel stage, made its first appearance in print in 1871. The triple grace note that begins this arrangement can be played in several different ways: You can pick the D, then hammer on the E and F# and pick the G. Or, starting with an up-pick, you can pick each grace note lightly, timing the figure to arrive correctly on the downbeat.

Words by Harry Birch
Music by William Gooch

Rachel:
Reuben, I have long been thinking,
What a good world this might be.
If the men were all transported,
Far beyond the Northern Sea.

Reuben:
Rachel, I have long been thinking,
What a fine world this might be.
If we had some more young ladies,
On this side the Northern Sea.

America, the Beautiful

Bates, a college English teacher, wrote these inspiring words after a visit to Colorado in the 1890s. Although many composers vied for the honor of setting them to music, they were found to be a perfect fit to Ward's 1882 hymn melody, "Materna," also called "O, Mother Dear, Jerusalem." And that's the way we know the song today.

Words by Katherine Lee Bates
Music by Samuel A. Ward

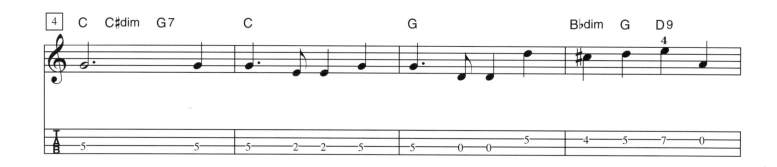

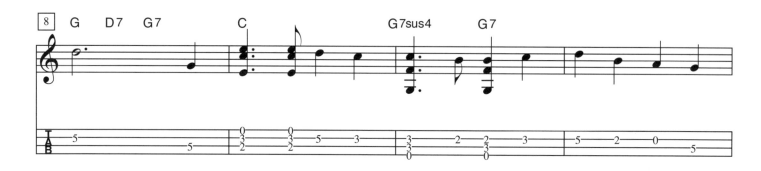

O beautiful for spacious skies, for amber waves of grain,
For purple mountain majesties above the fruited plain.
America! America! God shed his grace on thee,
And crown thy good with brotherhood,
From sea to shining sea.

The Girl I Left Behind Me

This tune is of Irish origin, but unlike many Gaelic tunes, is solidly based on the C major scale. It is often associated with the American Revolutionary War, during which it was very popular. Use downpicks for all the eighth notes and alternate picking for the 16ths.

Irish-American Dance Tune

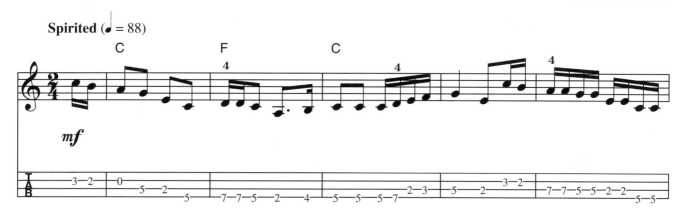

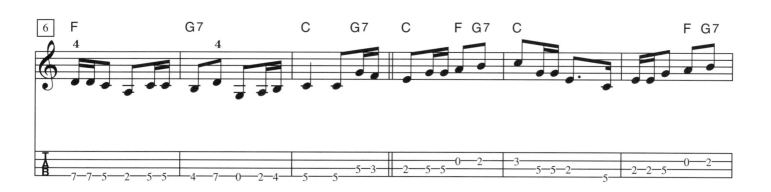

I am lonesome since I crossed the hill,
And o'er the moor and valley.
Such heavy thoughts my heart do fill
Since parting with my Sally.

Yankee Doodle Dandy

The original title of this patriotic classic was "The Yankee Doodle Boy." It was the high spot of George M. Cohan's *Little Johnny Jones*, a 1904 Broadway show that is given the credit for being the first modern American musical. Play it at a brisk march tempo and watch the fingering, especially the fill in measures 9 & 10. Also, note the clever way Cohan quotes from the original "Yankee Doodle" in measures 27–30.

Words and Music by
George M. Cohan

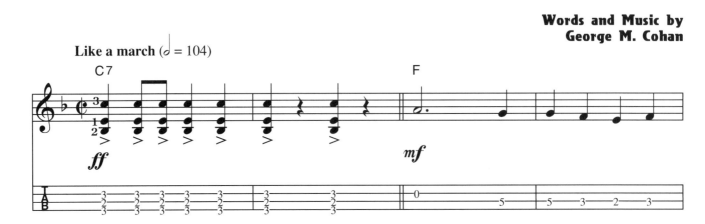

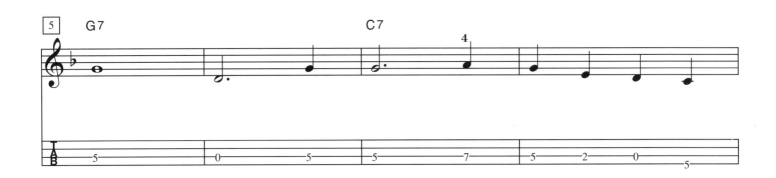

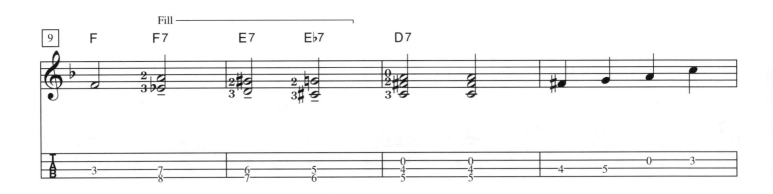

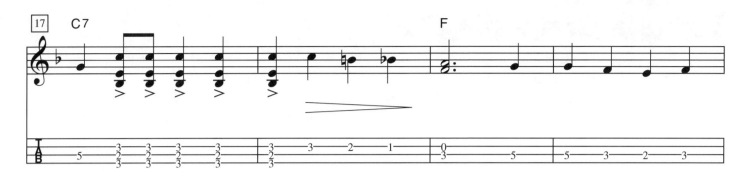

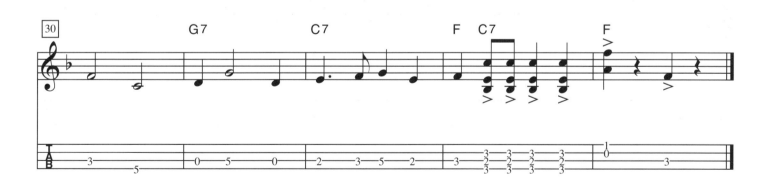

I'm a Yankee Doodle dandy,
A Yankee Doodle do or die,
A real live nephew of my Uncle Sam,
Born on the Fourth of July.
I've got a Yankee Doodle sweetheart,
She's my Yankee Doodle joy.
Yankee Doodle went to London just to ride the ponies,
I am that Yankee Doodle boy.

You're a Grand Old Flag

George M. Cohan was not only a patriot, but also a prolific songwriter and playwright. He was adept at using quotes from other songs in his own compositions; notice the way he smoothly interpolates "Auld Lang Syne" into this song in measures 26–30. (Also see comments on "Yankee Doodle Dandy.") Played up to the proper speed, the imitation bugle calls in measures 25 and 33 will take a little work, but your improved technique will make practicing them more than worth it.

**Word and Music by
George M. Cohan**

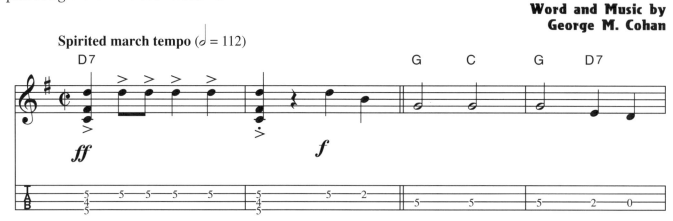

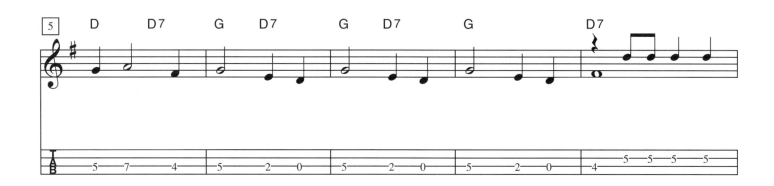

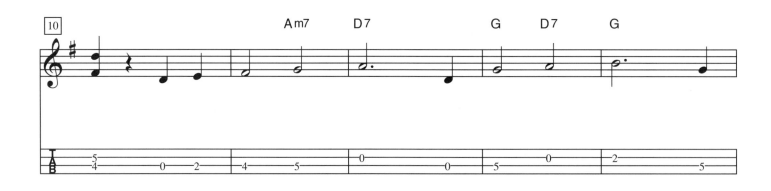

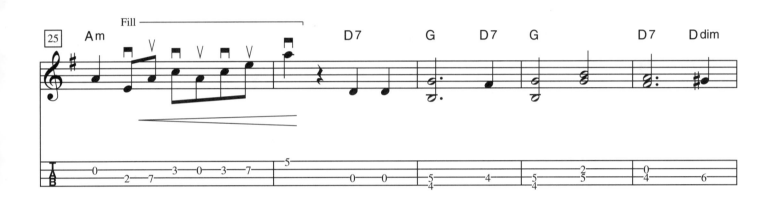

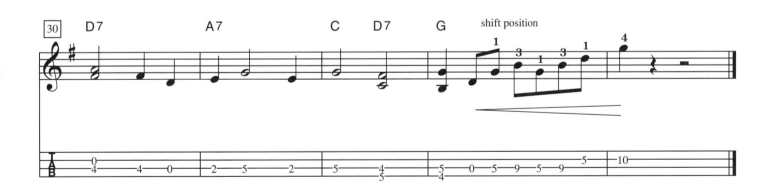

You're a grand old flag, you're a high-flying flag,
And forever in peace may you wave.
You're the emblem of the land I love,
The home of the free and the brave.

Ev'ry heart beats true under red, white and blue,
Where there's never a boast or brag.
But should auld acquanitance be forgot,
Keep your eye on the grand old flag.

When Johnny Comes Marching Home

One of the finest songs to come out of the American Civil War. The tune is probably of Irish origin which would explain its plaintive, modal quality. The song originally credited Louis Lambert as the composer; this was a pseudonym of Irish-born bandmaster Patrick Gilmore.

Patrick Gilmore

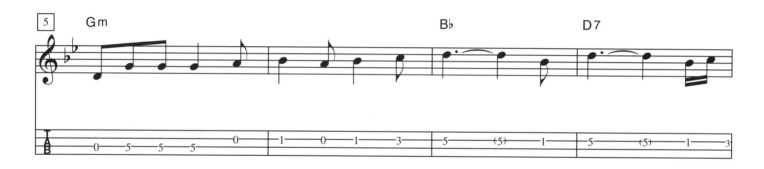

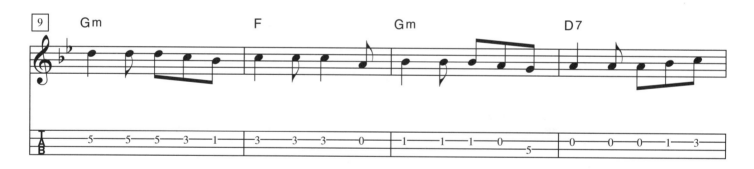

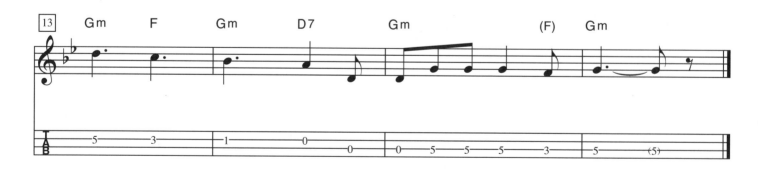

When Johnny comes marching home again, Hurrah! Hurrah!
We'll give him a hearty welcome then, Hurrah! Hurrah!
The men will cheer, the boys will shout,
The ladies, they will all turn out,
And we'll all feel gay when Johnny comes marching home.

Beautiful Brown Eyes

This western ballad has two examples (measures 2 and 10) of a type of chromatic harmony that later became known as "barbershop." Keep at least one finger down when moving from chord to chord. This will give the chord changes the smooth, connected sound called legato (le-GAH-toe).

Cowboy Song

Beautiful, beautiful brown eyes,
I loved you but all in vain.
Beautiful, beautiful brown eyes,
I'll never love blue eyes again.

Bile Them Cabbage Down

This high-spirited country tune works well on the mandolin. Strive for a rich, clear tone on the full chords and bring out the melody, which is always the highest note of the chord.

Country Tune

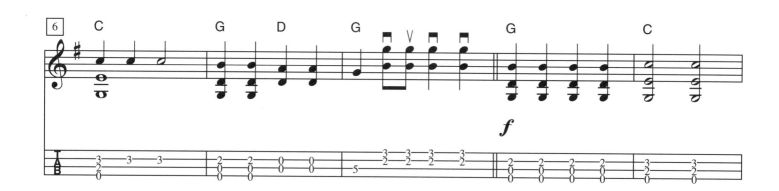

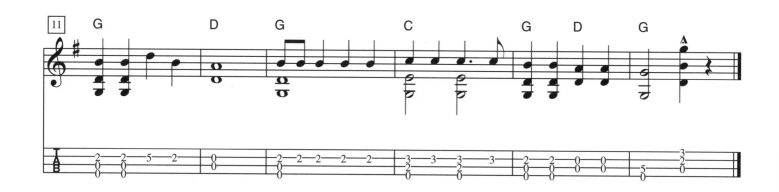

Verse:
Once I had an old gray mule, his name was Simon Slick;
He'd roll his eyes and back his ears, how that mule could kick!

Chorus:
Bile them cabbage down, boy, bile them cabbage down,
Craziest song I ever heard was "Bile Them Cabbage Down."

Bury Me Not on the Lone Prairie

Published in 1850 as "The Ocean Burial," the original words "O! bury me not in the deep, deep sea" were changed by some anonymous cowboy to reflect the hard life on the open range. Use tremolo to sustain the long notes, downpicks on the quarter notes, and alternate picking on the eighth notes.

Words: Anonymous
Music by George N. Allen

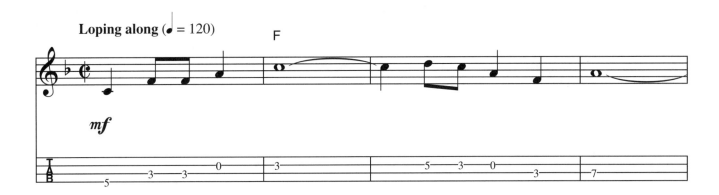

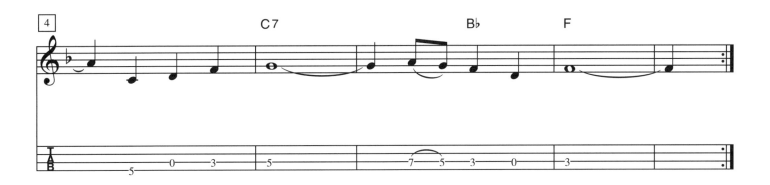

"Oh, bury me not on the lone prairie,"
These words came low and mournfully
From the ashen lips of a youth who lay,
On his dying bed at the close of day.

"Oh, bury me not on the lone prairie,
Where the coyotes howl and the wind blows free.
In a narrow grave just six by three,
Oh, bury me not on the lone prairie."

Home on the Range

This song, perhaps the most famous of all cowboy ballads, was composed in the 1870s but not copyrighted until 1905. Fills and slides add interest to this arrangement. When using tremolo on chords, pick the whole chord on the downbeat, but only tremolo on the top note for a cleaner sound.

Words by Dr. Brewster M. Higley
Music by Daniel E. Kelley

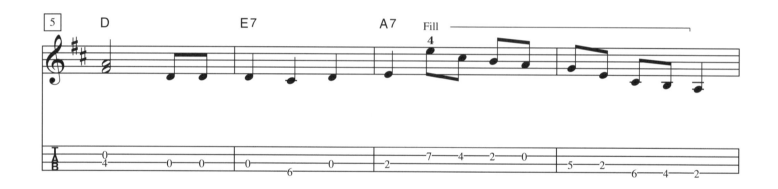

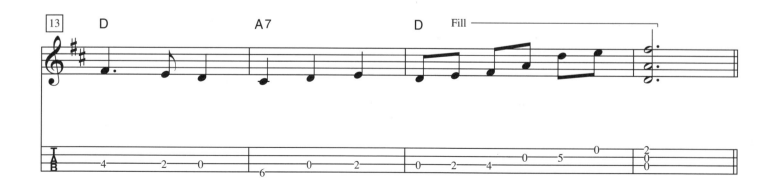

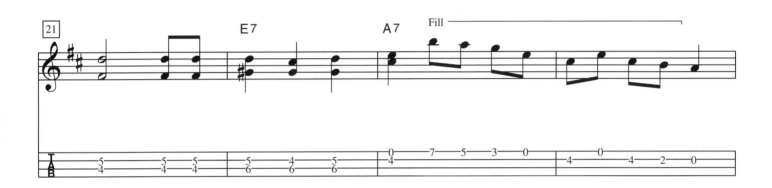

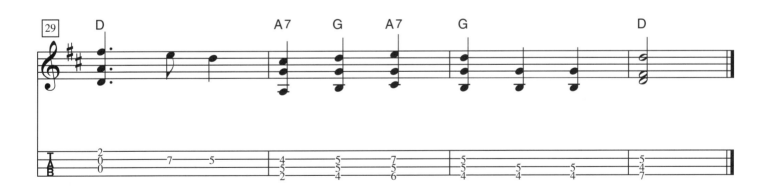

Verse:
Oh, give me a home where the buffalo roam,
Where the deer and the antelope play:
Where seldom is heard a discouraging word,
And the skies are not cloudy all day.

Chorus:
Home, home on the range,
Where the deer and the antelope play;
Where seldom is heard a discouraging word,
And the skies are not cloudy all day.

Jesse James

Here is another western ballad that glorifies killers and bank robbers. Note the line "...that dirty little coward who shot Mister Howard." Howard was one of Jesse's aliases, and it is typical of this type of song to make the criminal the hero and the lawman the villain. It makes a great bluegrass number, though.

American Folk Song

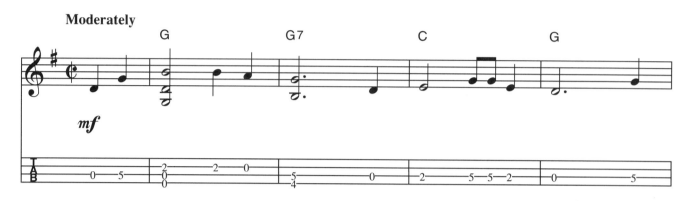

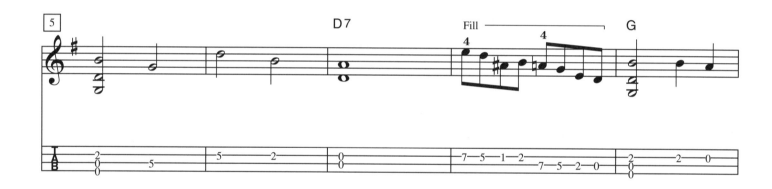

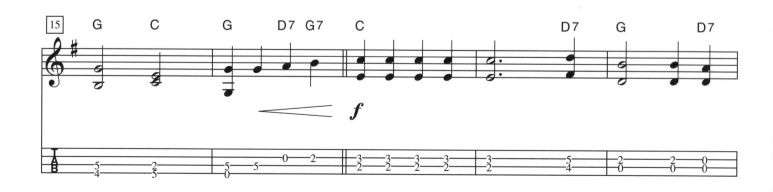

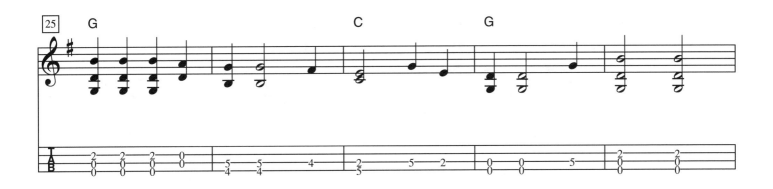

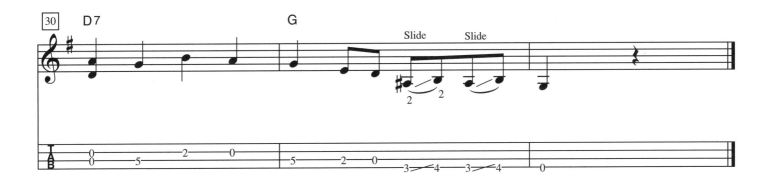

Jesse James was a lad who killed many a man,
He robbed the Glendale train.
And he stole from the rich and he gave to the poor,
With a hand and a heart and a brain.
Now Jesse had a wife to mourn for his life;
Three children, they were brave.
(They were brave.)
But that dirty little coward who shot Mister Howard,
Has laid poor Jesse in his grave.

John Hardy

This is just one of the many songs that tells the story of a desperado. Don't let the one-sharp key signature fool you. The song is based on a transposed Mixolydian mode, which is a fancy way of saying that the Mixolyian mode (G A B C D E F) has been transposed up five steps to D (D E F♯ G A B C).

American Folk Song

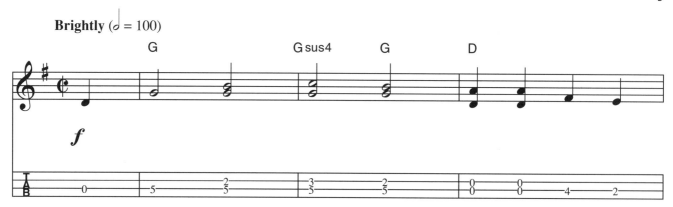

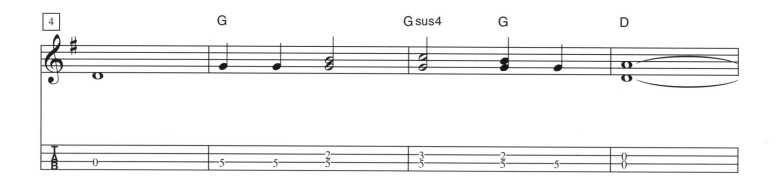

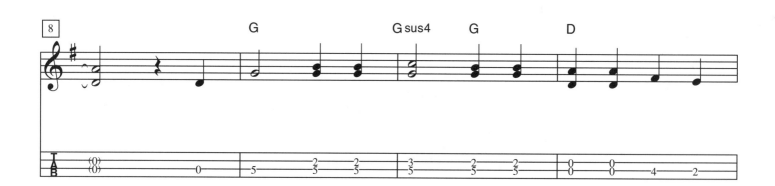

John Hardy was a des'prate little man,
Carried two guns ev'ry day.
He shot him a man on the West Virginia line,
Ought to see John Hardy get away, poor boy,
You ought to see John Hardy get away.

He went on across to the East Stone Bridge,
There he thought he'd be free.
But up steps the sheriff and takes him by the arm,
Says, "Johnny, come along with me," poor boy,
"Johnny come along with me."

He sent for his mama and his papa, too,
To come and go his bail,
But there wasn't no bail on a murder charge,
So they threw John Hardy back in jail, poor boy,
They threw John Hardy back in jail.

I've been to the east and I've been to the west,
Traveled this wide world round.
Been to the river and I've been baptized,
But now I'm on my hangin' ground, Lord, Lord,
Now I'm on my hangin' ground.

The Wabash Cannonball

A country classic, this is one of the many great songs inspired by railroads. "The Wreck of the Old 97," "Casey Jones," and, of course, "I've Been Workin' on the Railroad" also come to mind. Use tremolo only on notes that are at least two beats long.

Old-time Fiddle Tune

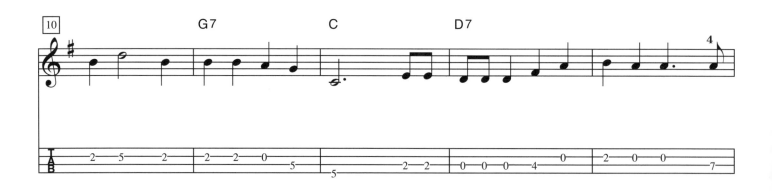

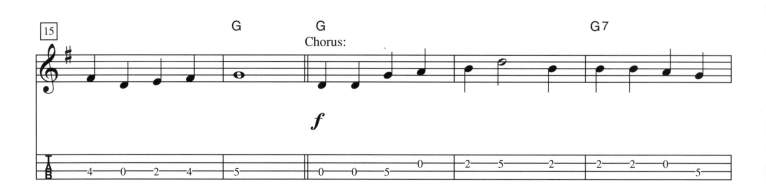

Verse:
From the great Atlantic Ocean to the wide Pacific shore,
The queen of flowing rivers to the southland by the door,
She's tall and dark and handsome and known quite well by all;
She's the regular combination of the Wabash Cannonball.

Chorus:
Listen to the jingle, the rumble and the roar,
As you glide along the woodlands, o'er the hills and by the shore.
Hear the mighty rush of engine, hear the lonesome whistle's squall,
As you travel 'cross the country on the Wabash Cannonball.

Bessarabian Horra

Bessarabia is a district in western Ukraine and Rumania. Because it was a gateway to western Europe, its population was influenced by many different Eastern and near-Eastern cultures as this exotic melody shows. In measures 9 and 10, the D# to E grace notes are played on the 2nd string while sounding the open 1st string. Double grace notes, such as those in measures 2 and 6 are played as hammer-ons and pull-offs. A *horra* is a Jewish circle-dance.

Jewish Folk Dance

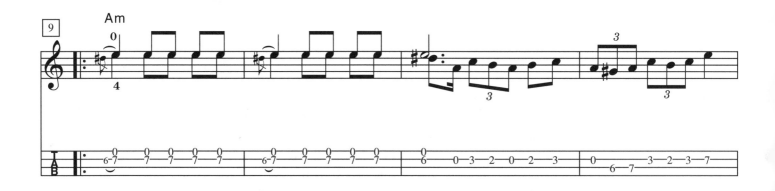

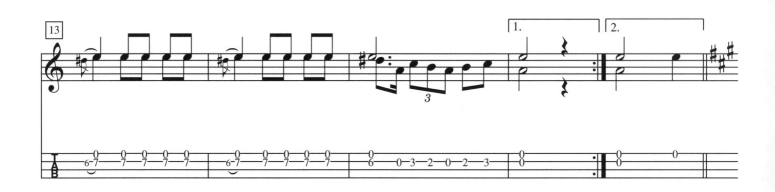

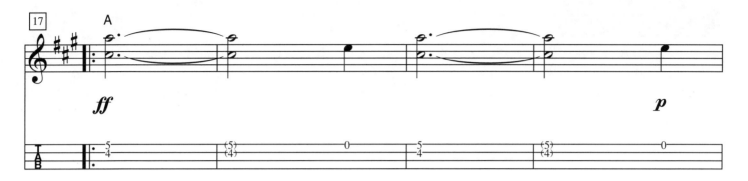

gradually getting louder till the end

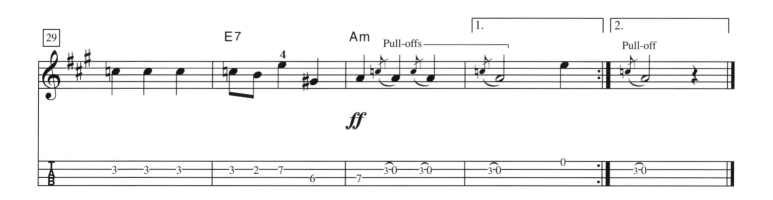

Hava Nagila

This composition is heard at virtually every Jewish celebration. It uses the G harmonic minor scale: G A B♭ C D E♭ F♯, stressing, rather than avoiding, the interval of the augmented 2nd (E♭ to F♯). For an authentic performance, play it through the first time at a moderate tempo, the second time faster and the final time faster still. This is an exuberant dance in duple meter called a hora, not to be confused with the Bessarabian horra, which is in triple meter.

Traditional Jewish Dance

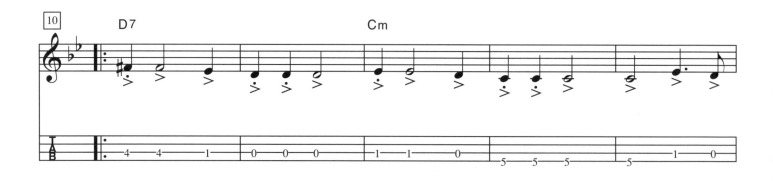

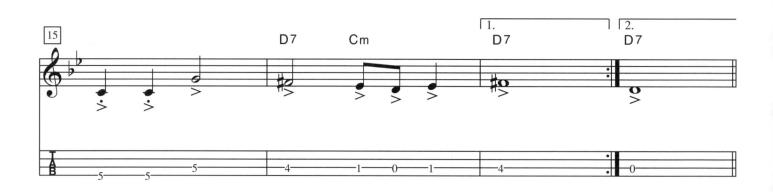

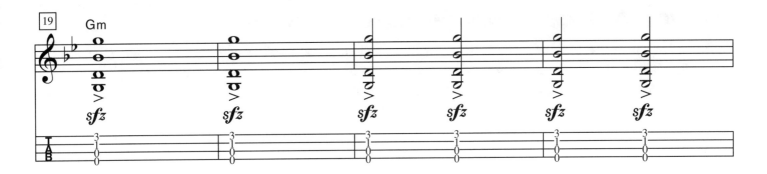

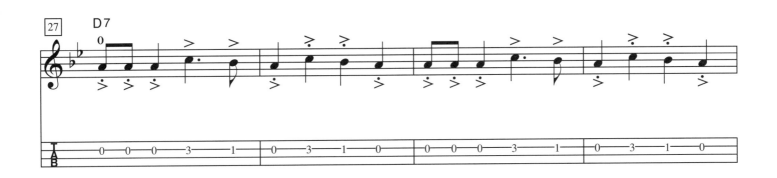

Waves of the Danube (Anniversary Song)

The melody, which dates from the late 19th century, was well known at Jewish weddings and anniversary parties in the 1940s when Al Jolson's voice was featured in a film about his life. A set of words was written for the movie, and the title was changed to "Anniversary Song." Use plenty of tremolo and watch the fingering, especially beginning with measure 18 where the eighth-note run puts you in position for the subsequent passage in thirds.

Ion Ivanovici

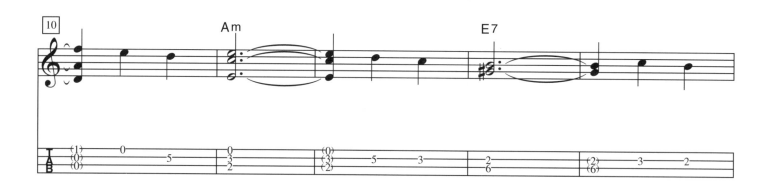

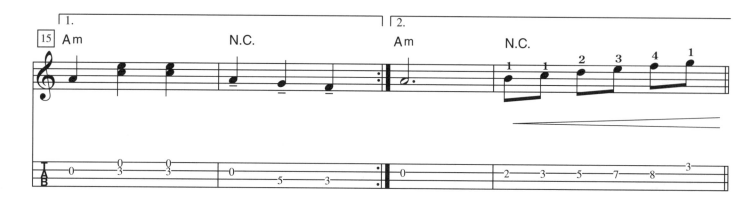

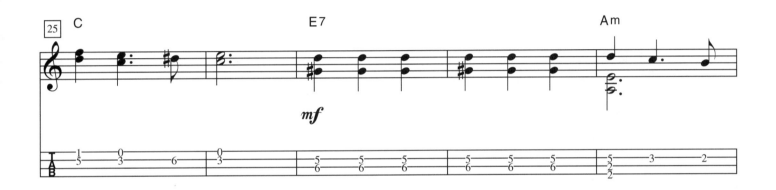

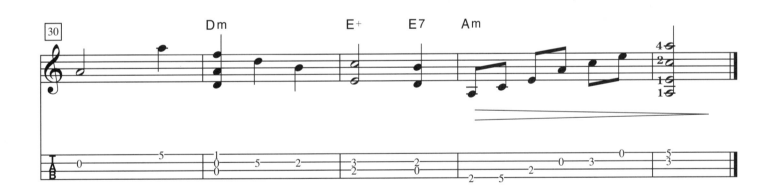

Chosen Kalle Mazel Tov

This sprightly dance tune is played at virtually every Jewish wedding. The title translates (more or less) into "Good Luck to the Bride and Groom." This arrangement takes advantage of the fact that the note A can be played either open or on the 3rd string, 7th fret. See measures 1, 5, and especially 13 and 14 where the two As are played simultaneously.

Traditional Jewish Dance

Careless Love

To give this tune a bluesy feel, play the eighth notes with a swing feel by making the downbeat eighth-notes slightly longer than the upbeat eighth-notes. Use tremolo on the long notes. To play the grace note in measure 4, finger the A♯ with the 2nd finger, then pick the string and quickly slide the finger up one fret to the B without picking again.

Traditional Blues

Love, oh love, oh careless love,
Love, oh love, oh careless love,
Love, oh love, oh careless love,
Just see, what love has done to me.

(Continue similarly)
Cried last night and the night before, (3 times)
I'll cry tonight and cry no more.

When I wore my apron low (3 times)
You'd follow me through rain and snow.

Now I wear my apron high (3 times)
You see my door and pass on by.

Don't Let Your Deal Go Down

There are many slides in this arrangement. When they occur on the low D, you must finger this note on the 4th string, 7th fret, because it is impossible to slide up to an open note. Also notice that on the first chord, a G chord missing the third (the note B), the 3rd and 2nd fingers both play on the 5th fret. Players with large fingers may have a problem with this, in which case they can use a regular G chord instead.

American Folk Song

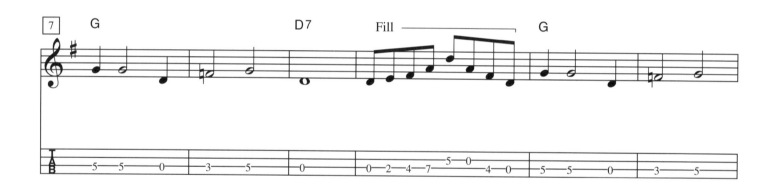

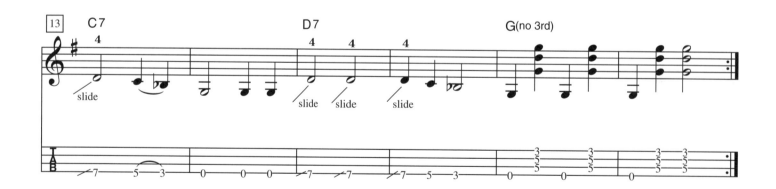

Don't let your deal go down, down, down,
Don't let your deal go down.
Don't let your deal go down, down, down,
Till your last gold dollar is gone.

Goin' Down the Road Feelin' Bad

This typical country blues tune was written by an anonymous singer about a life of poverty that most of us can't even imagine. Use the 2nd finger to play the slides from B# (the same as C) to C#. The fills are sometimes called the "church lick."

American Folk Blues

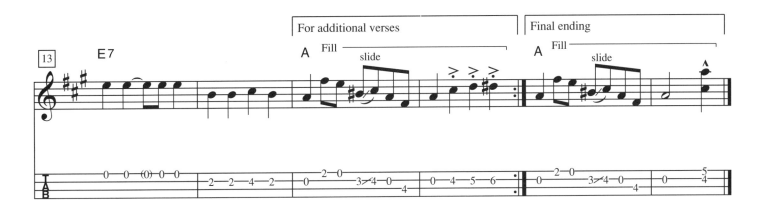

I'm goin' down the road feelin' bad, Lord, Lord,
I'm goin' down the road feelin' bad,
I'm goin' down the road feelin' bad, Lord, Lord,
And I ain't gonna be treated thisaway.

(Cont. similarly)
I'm goin' where the climate suits my clothes...

I'm down in the jailhouse on my knees...

Hard, Ain't It Hard

Play this classic country blues using tremolo sparingly, perhaps only on the half notes and longer notes.
The fill-ins in this arrangement use full chords.

American Folk Blues

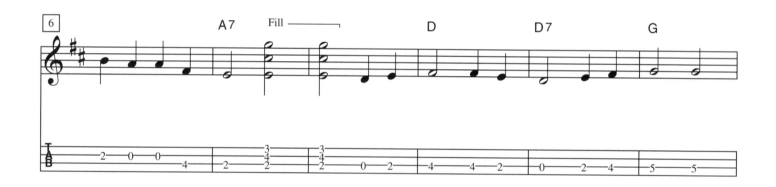

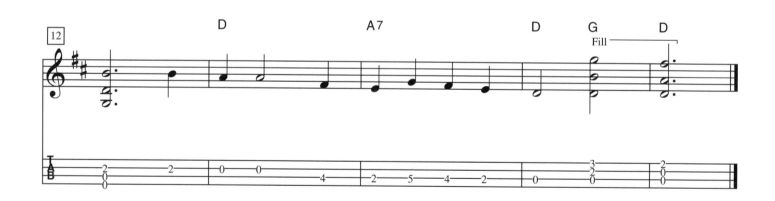

It's hard, and it's hard, ain't it hard,
To love one who never will love you.
Well, it's hard, and it's hard, ain't it hard, real hard,
To love one who never will be true.

Pick a Bale o' Cotton

This work song has many repeated notes, making it a lot of fun to play on the mandolin. Notice the contrasts in dynamics starting at measure 5 which—if you execute them accurately—will add a lot of interest to your playing.

African-American Work Song

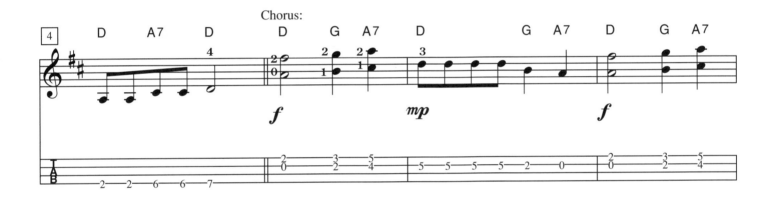

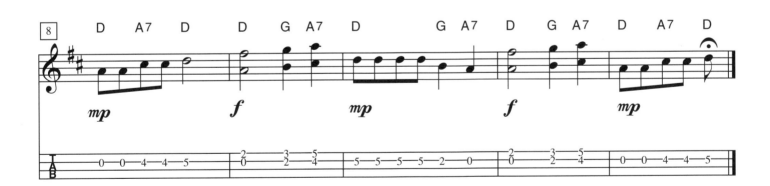

Verse:
You gotta jump down, turn around,
Pick a bale o' cotton.
Jump down, turn around,
Pick a bale a day.

Chorus:
Oh, Lawdy! pick a bale o' cotton.
Oh, Lawdy, pick a bale a day.
Oh, Lawdy! pick a bale o' cotton.
Oh, Lawdy, pick a bale a day.

Salty Dog

This arrangement features many full-sounding chords, which shouldn't give you much trouble if you follow the TAB and the fingering. A salty dog was 19th century slang for a great lover. Most of the verses to this song are unprintable.

African-American Folk Song

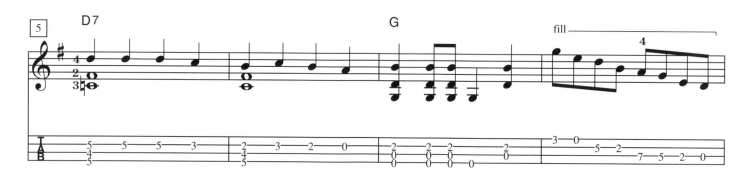

Salty Dog, Salty Dog,
I don't wanna be your man at all,
Honey, let me be your Salty Dog.

Down in the wildwood sittin' on a log,
Singin' a song about a salty dog.
Honey, let me be your Salty Dog.

Come All Ye Fair and Tender Ladies

This melody is based on a D minor hexachord (six-note scale): D E F G A C. The use of this ancient mode, which predates the development of the major and minor scales, supports the theory that most Appalachian tunes were brought over from England, Scotland, and Ireland by the very first settlers in the 16th and 17th centuries.

American Folk Song

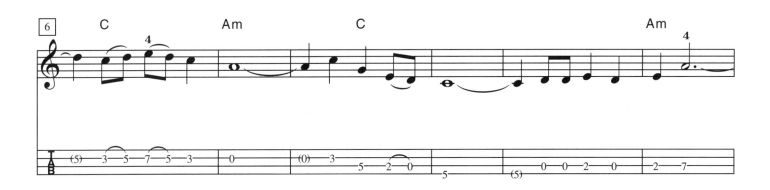

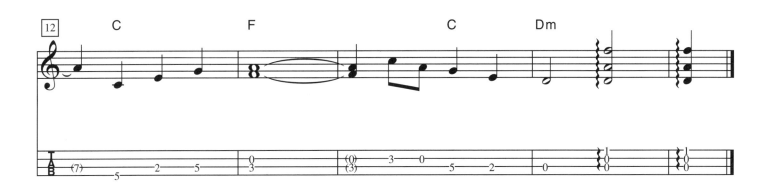

Come all ye fair and tender ladies,
Be careful how you court young men.
They're like the stars of a summer's evening,
First they appear, then they're gone again.

The Cuckoo

This very pretty folk song is of British origin. Notes that are slurred together, such as the first two notes of measure 1, should be connected as smoothly as possible. Notes with a staccato dot are cut off short.

American Folk Song

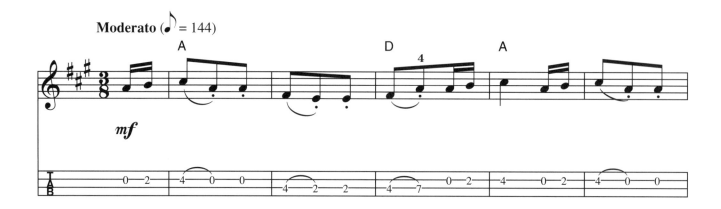

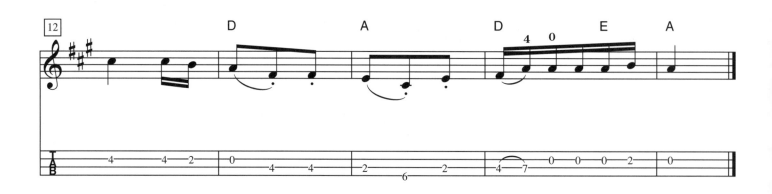

Down in the Valley

Also called "Birmingham Jail," both versions tell of a sad longing for another time and place. Use tremolo on the longer notes and see how pretty you can make the fill-in chords sound in measures 6 and 12.

American Folk Song

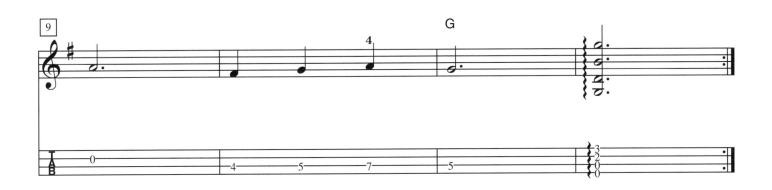

Down in the valley, the valley so low,
Hang your head over, hear the wind blow.
Hear the wind blow, dear, hear the wind blow.
Hang your head over, hear the wind blow.

Roses love sunshine, vi'lets love dew,
Angels in heaven know I love you.
Build me a castle forty feet high,
So I can see her (him) as she (he) goes by.

The Drunken Sailor

Life on the old sailing ships was incredibly demanding, both mentally and physically. Sailors used chanteys like this one to help them work together, especially when raising the sails (hence, the words "hooray and up she rises"). The melody is based on an ancient scale called the Dorian mode, which consists of the notes D E F G A B C. To make it easier to play, in this arrangement the mode is transposed up a whole tone, E F♯ G A B C♯ D.

Traditional Sea Chantey

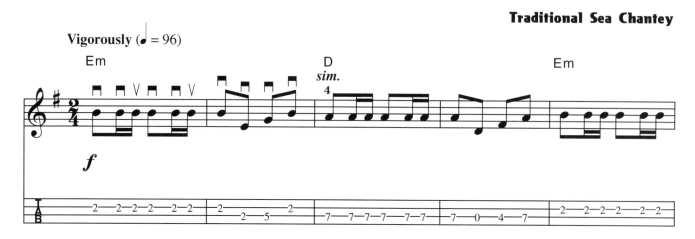

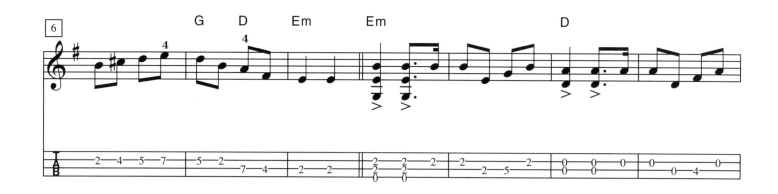

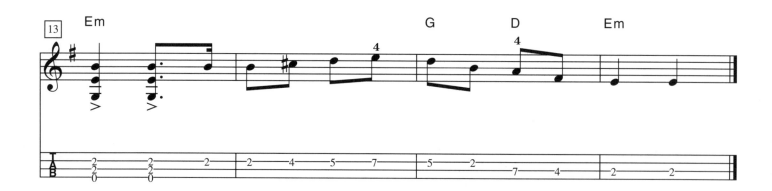

What shall we do with a drunken sailor? (3 times)
Earlye in the morning.

Hooray, and up she rises, (3 times)
Earlye in the morning.

Man of Constant Sorrow

This country classic played an important role in the recent film *O Brother, Where Art Thou?*, a modern take on *The Odyssey* set in Depression-era Appalachia. Use tremolo only on the long notes, and play the arrangement very rhythmically.

American Folk Song

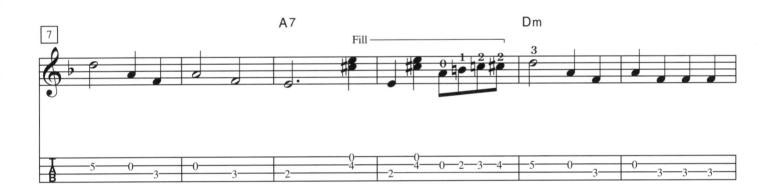

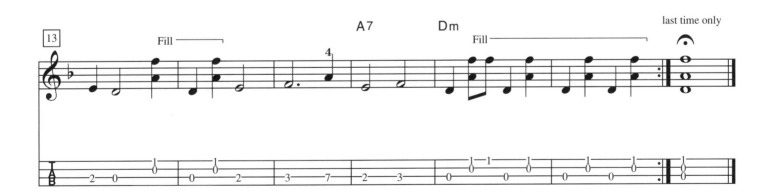

I'm a man of constant sorrow,
I've seen trouble all my days.
I left my home in old Kentucky,
Where I was born and raised.

I'm a man of constant sorrow,
A stranger in ev'ry town.
Friends, I have none to give me comfort,
While I go roaming 'round.

In the Pines

This is one of the finest of the Appalachian songs. The lyric is forceful and the melody shows how a moving and powerful musical statement can be made using only a tetrachord, the four notes G, Bb, C, and D. The great folksinger Leadbelly recorded his version in the 1940s and the Nirvana frontman Kurt Cobain sang his version to tremendous effect before his unfortunate suicide in 1994.

Appalachian Folk Song

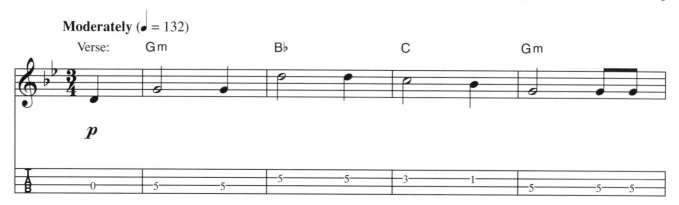

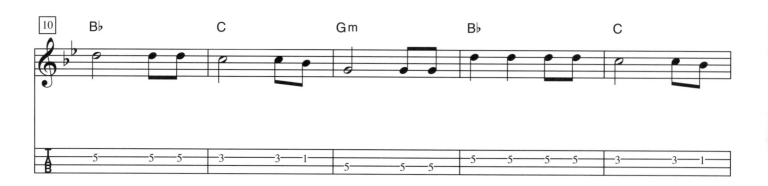

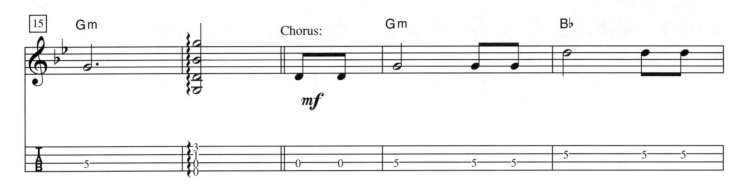

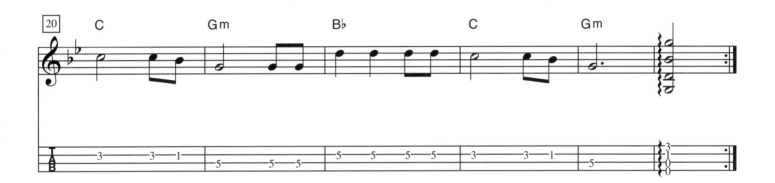

Verse:
True love, true love, don't lie to me,
Tell me where did you sleep last night?
I slept in the pines,
Where the sun never shines,
And I shivered when the cold wind blowed.

Chorus:
In the pines, in the pines,
Where the sun never shines,
And I shivered when the cold wind blowed.

Verse:
Tell me, where did you get them pretty little shoes,
And the dress you wear so fine?
I got my shoes from a railroad man,
Got my dress from a driver in the mine.
(repeat Chorus)

Verse:
I wish to the Lord I'd-a never been born,
Or died when I was young.
I never would of kissed your sweet lips,
Nor heard your rattling tongue.
(repeat Chorus)

Poor Wayfaring Stranger (Wayfaring Stranger)

This arrangement of the beautiful, modal Appalachian song uses a modern harmonization. The ballad was originally sung *a cappella* (without accompaniment). Concentrate on tone and phrasing and tremolo the longer notes to see how much expression you can get into your performance.

Appalachian Folk Ballad

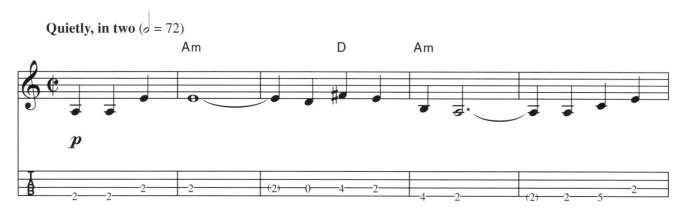

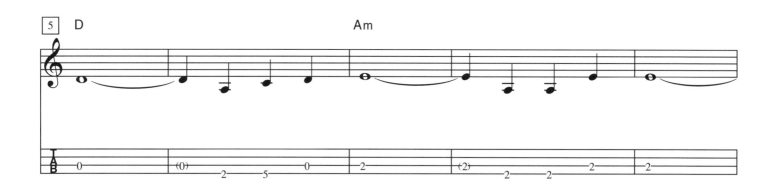

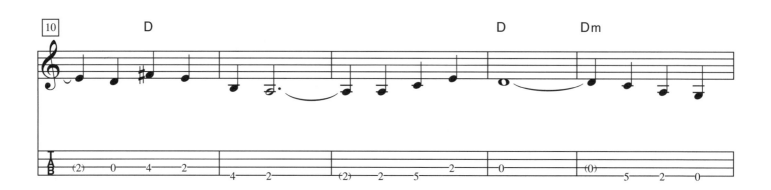

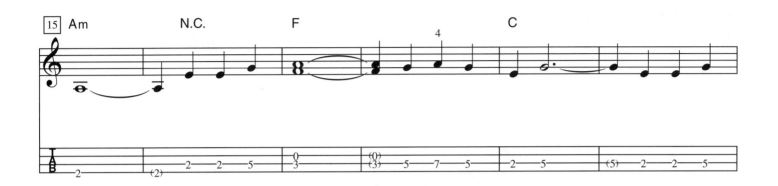

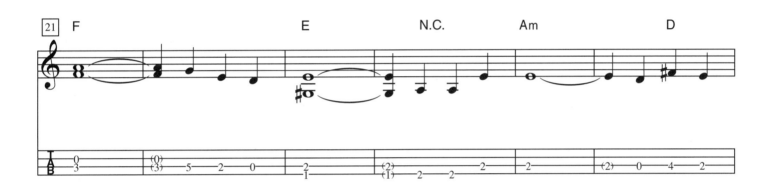

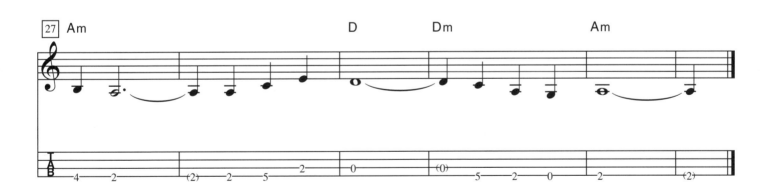

I am a poor wayfaring stranger,
A-trav'lin' through this world of woe.
But there's no sickness, toil or danger,
In that bright land to which I go.
I'm goin' home to see my mother,
I'm goin' there no more to roam.
I'm just a-goin' over Jordan,
I'm just a-goin' over home.

Nine Hundred Miles

This arrangement of a beautiful modal Appalachian ballad features several places where the melody is played entirely on the D string below the open A string. The A string acts like the drone on a bagpipe or the short, unfingered 5th string on a five-string banjo.

American Folk Song

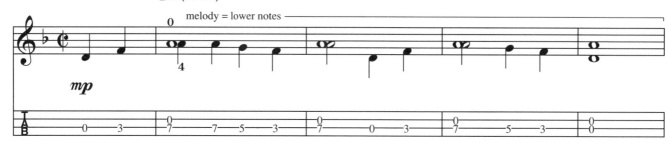

Well, I'm walking down the track, I've got tears in my eyes,
Tryin' to read a letter from my home.
And if this train runs me right I'll be home tomorrow night,
'Cause I'm nine hundred miles from my home,
And I hate to hear that lonesome whistle blow.

Shady Grove

The melody is often below the harmony in this arrangement which is based on the D minor hexachord (six-note scale): D E F G A C. Pay attention to measure 3 where the open A is played simultaneously with the A on the 3rd string, 7th fret.

American Folk Song

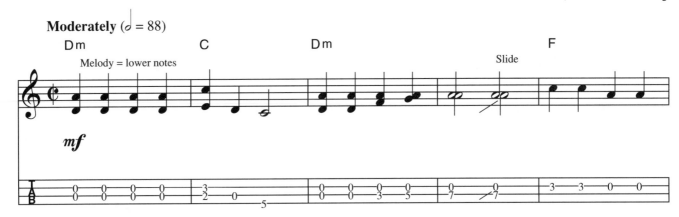

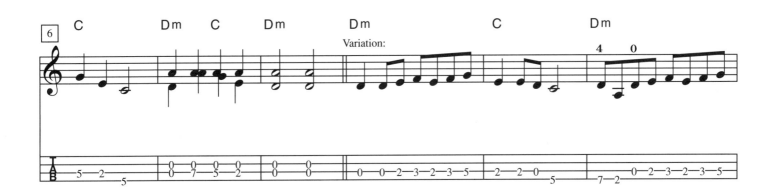

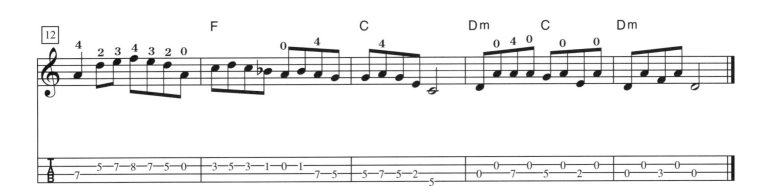

Verse:
Cheeks as red as a bloomin' rose,
Eyes of the deepest brown,
You are the darlin' of my heart,
Stay till the sun goes down.

Chorus:
Shady Grove, my true love,
Shady Grove I know;
Shady Grove, my true love,
Bound for Shady Grove.

Good Morning to All

This melody—possibly the most familiar in the world—may have been derived from a Negro spiritual that the Hill sisters, teachers and musicologists, discovered in their research. This is the original 1893 version which appeared in a collection called *Song Stories for the Kindergarten*. The version that we all know appeared in 1924. A lawsuit established the copyright in 1934 after "Happy Birthday to You" was included in a movie under the mistaken impression that it was a folk song.

Words by Patty and Mildred Hill
Music: Negro Spiritual

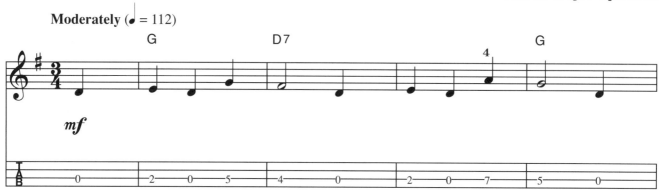

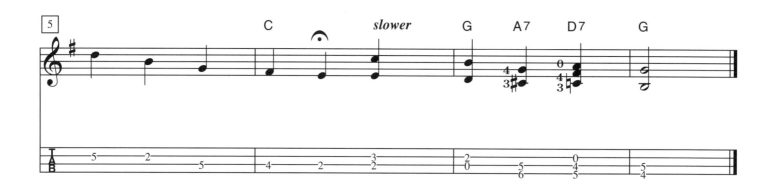

Good morning to you,
Good morning to you,
Good morning, dear children,
Good morning to you.

Hush, Little Baby

Many a child in pioneer days was lulled to sleep with this song. Children still love it. This arrangement uses two-note harmony throughout. See if you can bring out the melody, which is always the top note.

American Folk Song

Hush, little baby, don't say a word,
Poppa's gonna buy you a mockingbird.

And if that mockingbird won't sing,
Poppa's gonna buy you a golden ring.

And if that golden ring turns to brass,
Poppa's gonna buy you a looking glass.

And if that looking glass gets broke,
Poppa's gonna buy you a billy goat.

And if that billy goat won't pull,
Poppa's gonna buy you a cart and bull.

And if that cart and bull turn over,
Poppa's gonna buy you a doggie named Rover.

And if that dog named Rover won't bark,
Poppa's gonna buy you a horse and cart.

And if that horse and cart fall down,
You'll still be the sweetest little baby in town.

The Itsy Bitsy Spider

We don't know of a single child who doesn't love this song and the finger play that goes with it.
The melody was also the basis for a song of Australian origin called "Down by the Station."

Children's Fingerplay Song

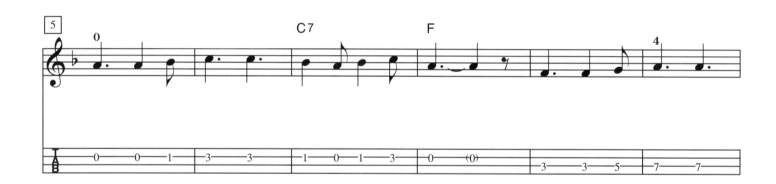

The itsy bitsy spider went up the waterspout,
Down came the rain and washed the spider out,
Out came the sun and dried up all the rain,
And the itsy bitsy spider climbed up the spout again.

Old MacDonald's Farm

Also known as "Old MacDonald Had a Farm," the words of this familiar children's song are derived from an early 18th-century British opera, *Wonders of the Sun or Kingdom of the Birds* by Thomas D'Urfey. The original music was different, however, and the song we know today developed in America during the 19th century and was first published in 1917.

American Folk Song

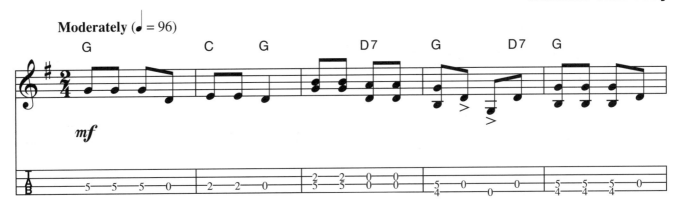

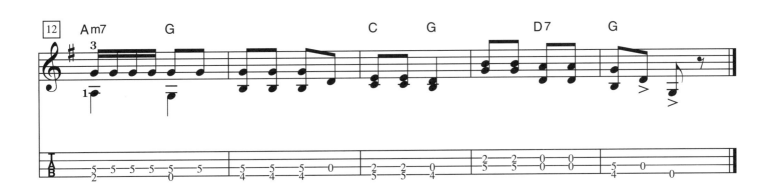

Old MacDonald had a farm, ee-i-ee-i-o!
And on this farm he had a cow, ee-i-ee-i-o.
With a moo moo here and a moo moo there,
Here a moo, there a moo, ev'rywhere a moo moo,
Old MacDonald had a farm, ee-i-ee-i-o!

(continue similarly)
pig...oink
horse...neigh
dog...ruff
cat...meow
etc.

Polly Wolly Doodle

This nonsense song works well on the mandolin. Even if you read music well, consult the TAB for special fingering used in this arrangement. Most of the melody can and should be played entirely on the 3rd string. Going out of the open position avoids a lot of tricky picking, skipping strings, and jumping backward over a string after a downpick.

Origin unknown

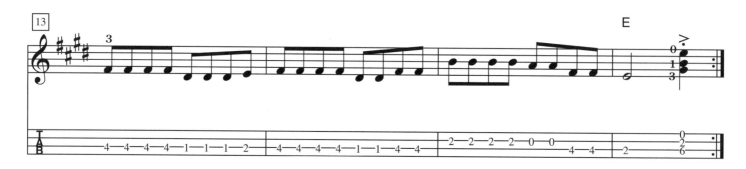

Verse:
Oh, I went down South for to see my Sal,
Singing Polly Wolly Doodle all the day.
My Sal she is a spunky gal,
Singing Polly Wolly Doodle all the day.

Chorus:
Fare thee well, fare thee well,
Fare thee well, my fairy fey,
For I'm goin' to Lou'sianna for to see
    my Susyanna,
Singing Polly Wolly Doodle all the day.

Verse:
Oh, my Sal she is a maiden fair,
Singing Polly Wolly Doodle all the day.
With curly eyes and laughing hair,
Singing Polly Wolly Doodle all the day.
(repeat Chorus)

Pop! Goes the Weasel

This famous tune is often played for a Virginia reel. Children love it, too, although the meaning of the original English words is somewhat obscure. "Pop" was British slang for "pawn." A "weasel" was not an animal, but a tool used by hatmakers. Thus, "a penny for a spool of thread, a penny for a needle," and the hatmaker must pawn his tools to make ends meet. But in the American version, the weasel is definitely an animal.

English Children's Song

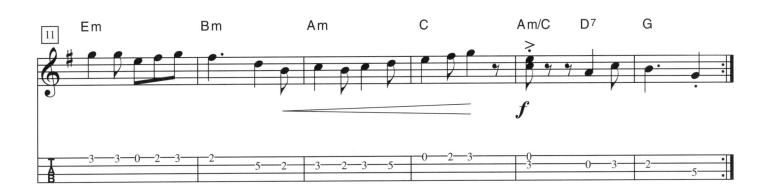

Around and 'round the cobbler's bench,
The monkey chased the weasel.
The monkey thought 'twas all in fun;
Pop! goes the weasel.

A penny for a spool of thread,
A penny for a needle.
That's the way the money goes;
Pop! goes the weasel.

This Old Man

This somewhat obscure English children's counting song, "This Old Man" became very well known after it was sung to a group of children by Ingrid Bergman in the 1958 film, "The Inn of the Sixth Happiness." In recent years (with a new set of words) it has become the theme of the popular children's TV show, "Barney & Friends."

Children's Song

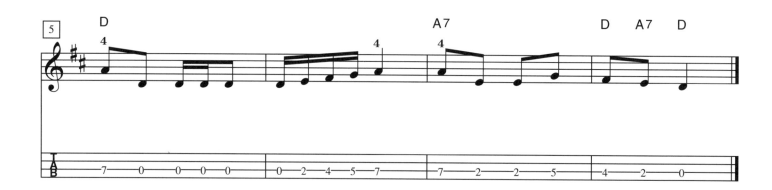

This old man,
He played one,
He played knick-knack on my thumb,
With a knick-knack, paddy whack,
Give a dog a bone;
This old man came rolling home.

(continue similarly)
...two...on my shoe...
...three...on my knee...
...four...on my door...
...five...sakes alive...
...six...many silly tricks...
...seven...up to heaven...
...eight...on my plate...
...nine...on my spine...
...ten...once again...

Deck the Halls

To play this carol at the fast tempo required, follow the tablature and fingering carefully.
They will help you avoid awkward picking and aid in producing a pleasing tone.

Traditional Welsh Carol

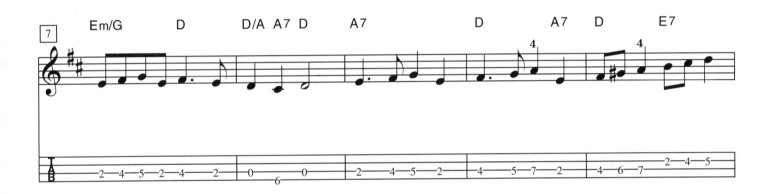

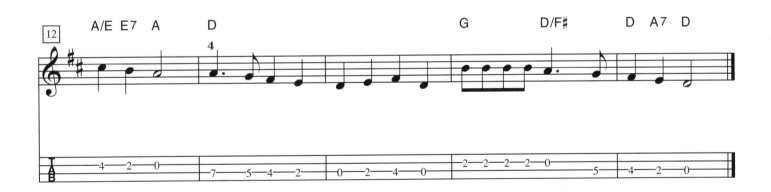

Deck the halls with boughs of holly,
Fa la la la la, la la la la.
'Tis the season to be jolly,
Fa la la la la, la la la la.
Don we now our gay apparel,
Fa la la, fa la la, la la la.
Troll the ancient Yuletide carol,
Fa la la la la, la la la la.

Jingle Bells

This cheerful ditty was written in the 1850s by an uncle of the famous financier, J. P. Morgan (the "P." stands for Pierpont). The song never mentions anything about Christmas and was originally intended for a Thanksgiving celebration, but the jingle bell rhythm was irresistible and so it lives on as a Christmas standard. Your performance will sound more professional if you play the staccato dots and tenuto dashes accurately.

**Words and Music by
James Pierpont**

Chorus:
Jingle bells! Jingle bells! Jingle all the way,
Oh, what fun it is to ride in a one-horse open sleigh.
Jingle bells! Jingle bells! Jingle all the way,
Oh, what fun it is to ride in a one-horse open sleigh

Verse:
Dashing through the snow in a one-horse open sleigh,
O'er the fields we go, laughing all the way.
Bells on bob-tail ring, making spirits bright;
Oh what fun to ride and sing a sleighing song tonight. Oh!
(Repeat Chorus)

Fum, Fum, Fum

Catalonia is a district in Spain with a culture that is quite different from mainstream Spanish culture. This lovely carol is written in the Catalonian dialect. The music is quite sophisticated for a folk tune, shifting from G minor to B♭ major and back to G minor.

Catalan Christmas Carol

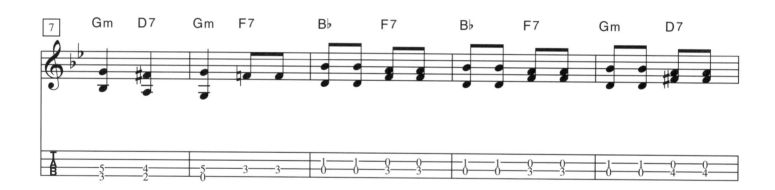

A vinticinc de desembre, fum, fum, fum.
A vinticinc de desembre, fum, fum, fum.
Ha nascut un min yonet ros i blanquet, ros i blanquet,
Fill de la Verge Maria n' és nat en una establia, fum, fum, fum.

Silent Night

Because the organ in his small Bavarian church was unusable, Gruber composed this beloved Christmas song in 1818 to be playable with three easy chords on the guitar. His tune may have been influenced by Rossini's opera *Semiramide*, which had just been written and which contains a melody similar to that of measures 11 and 12. Play this arrangement quietly and use tremolo sparingly.

Words by Joseph Mohr
Music by Franz Gruber

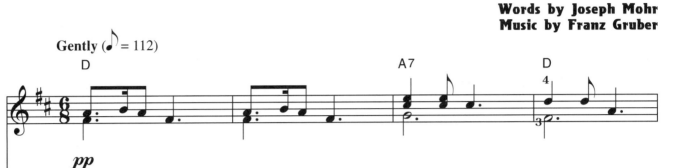

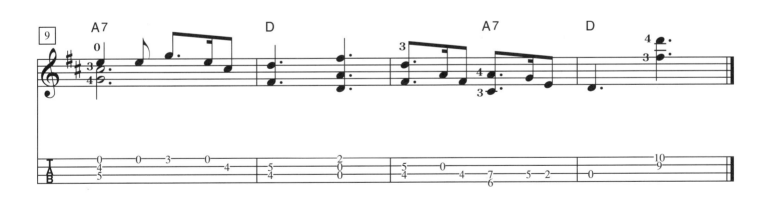

Silent night, holy night,
All is calm, all is bright.
'Round yon Virgin Mother and Child,
Holy Infant so tender and mild,
Sleep in heavenly peace;
Sleep in heavenly peace.

Catholic Boys

This Irish jig requires fast picking and nimble fingers. Although the Irish originally came to America as a despised minority, by the early 20th century they had used their native charm to great advantage and became important members of society, especially in law enforcement and politics. The music to this jig is found in a 1905 collection of dance tunes that every violinist of the time was expected to know.

Traditional Irish Jig

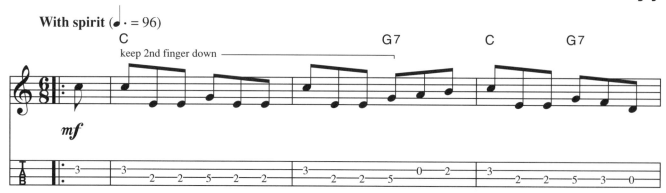

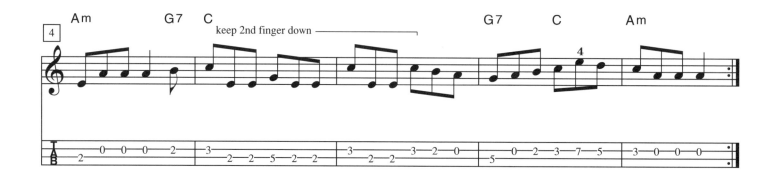

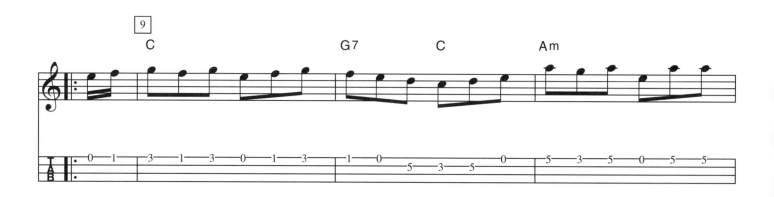

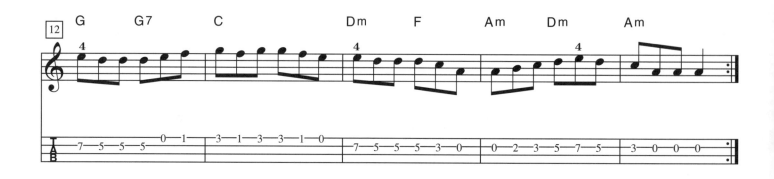

Danny Boy (Londonderry Air)

Some have called "Londonderry Air" the most beautiful melody ever written. Many sets of words were set to it, including one by the great Irish bard Thomas Moore, but only Weatherly's lyric is heard today. Ironically, he was an Englishman. Watch the fingering on this one. It will enable you to play the double-note passages smoothly.

Words by Fred Weatherly
Music: Traditional Irish Melody

Oh, Danny Boy, the pipes, the pipes are calling,
From glen to glen and down the mountainside.
The summer's gone, and all the roses falling,
It's you, it's you must go and I must bide.

But come ye back when summer's in the meadow,
Or when the valley's hushed and white with snow,
It's I'll be here in sunshine or in shadow;
Oh, Danny Boy, oh Danny Boy, I love you so!

Irish Washerwomen

This famous Virginia reel is a wonderful, spirited tune. It's also a fine technical exercise requiring nimble fingers and fast crosspicking.

Virginia Reel

Jeb Wilson's Clog Dance

Clog dancing is still popular, especially within the Irish-American culture. Play this typical example with a lilt.
Make sure the dotted-8th/16th-note figures are played accurately and not allowed to "soften" into broken triplets.

Irish Clog Dance

Paddy Whack

Here's a typical Irish tune, complete with fast 6/8 rhythms and a modal feeling throughout. "Paddy" was a generic name for an Irishman that was more than a little condescending. It derives from the habit of so many Irish parents naming their sons after St. Patrick, patron saint of Ireland.

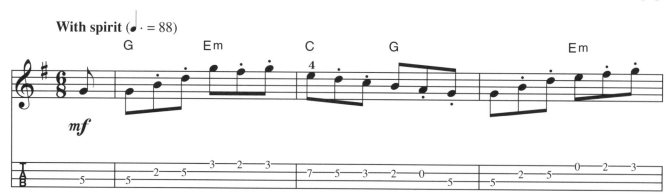

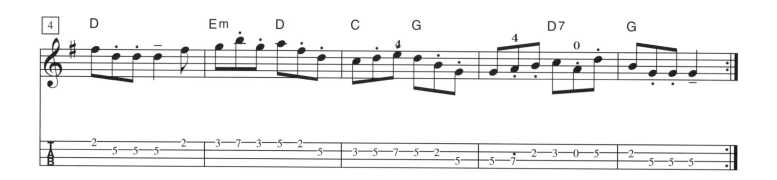

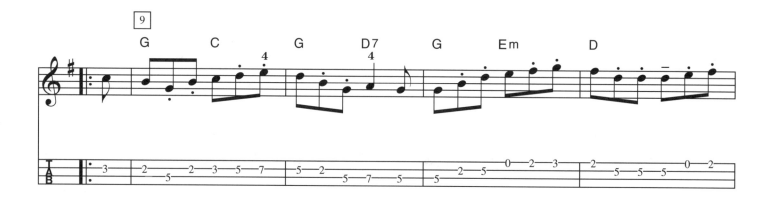

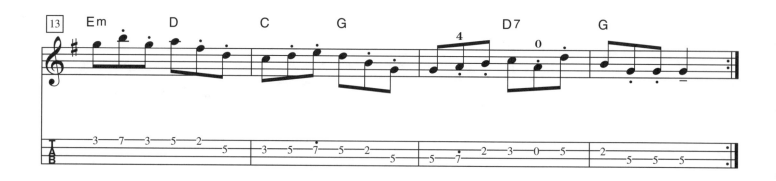

Rakes of Mallow

In this fast Irish dance, notice that the note A in measure 2 is played on the 2nd string with the 4th finger. The similar passage in measure 4 uses the open A. This is to avoid skipping backward over a string after a downpick.

Irish Dance

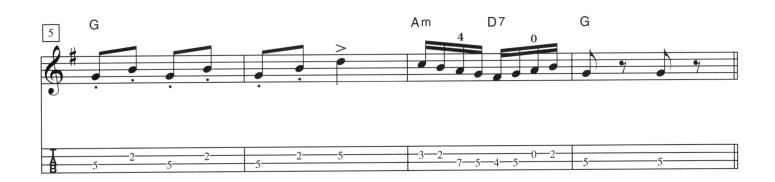

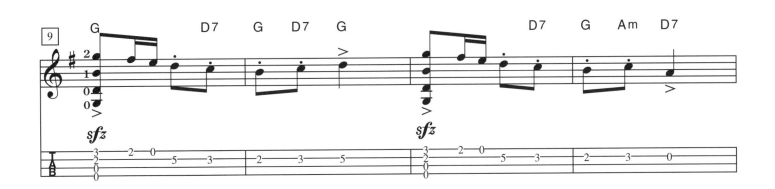

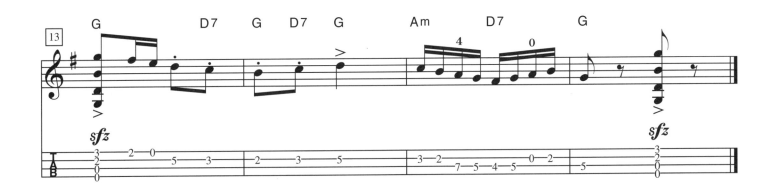

Stack o' Barley

Learning this jig is an absolute must if you're going to play Irish weddings or in any setting that features Irish dancing. It should be played briskly at 144 beats-per-minute or faster.

Irish Jig

Ode to Joy (from Symphony No. 9)

This melody, possibly a German folk song, is an important theme in Beethoven's stupendous Ninth Symphony. Amazingly, the great German master was completely deaf when he composed it, using a full chorus and orchestra and heralding the Romantic era in music. Play this arrangement at a brisk tempo, and make sure that the lower harmony notes don't overpower the higher melody.

Ludwig van Beethoven

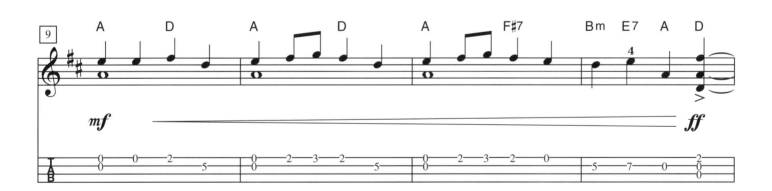

Jesu, Joy of Man's Desiring

The great contrapuntalist J. S. Bach was fond of contructing countermelodies to well-known tunes. This one is based on a 1642 Lutheran hymn by Johann Schopp—a snippet of which is included in measures 9–11. Each measure of the somewhat unusual 9/8 meter is played like three measures of 3/8 time.

Johann Sebastian Bach

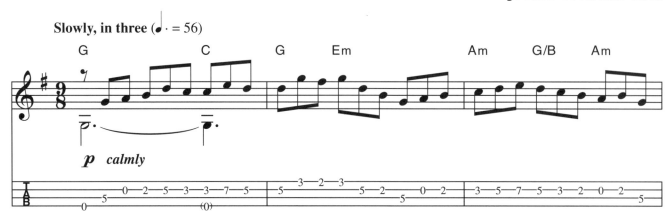

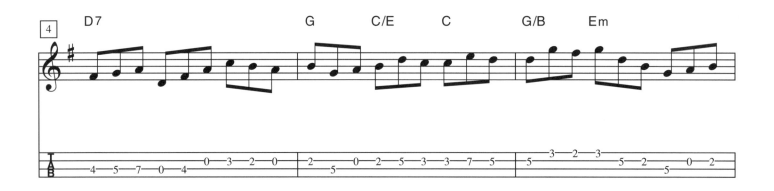

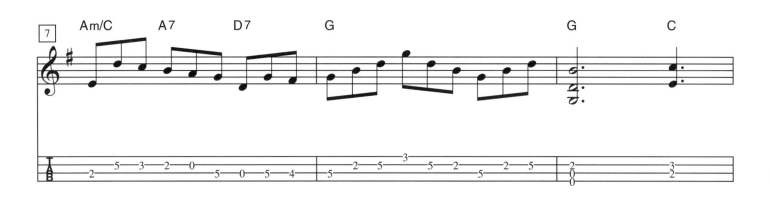

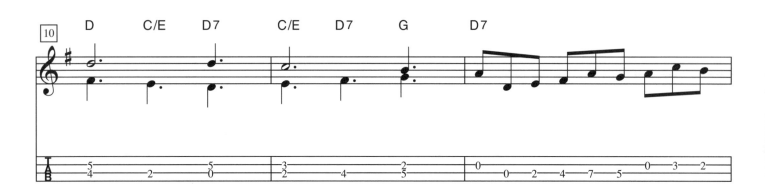

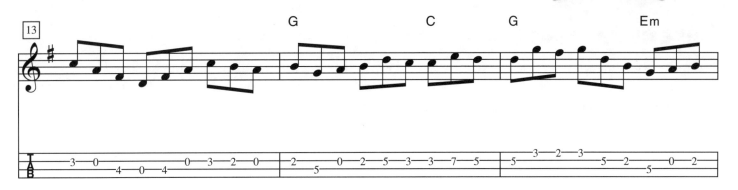

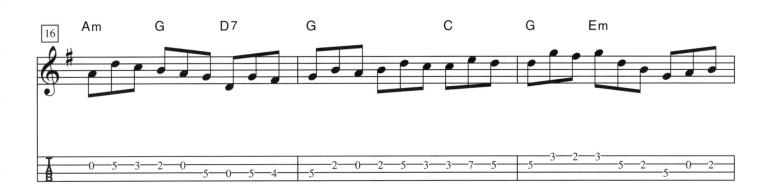

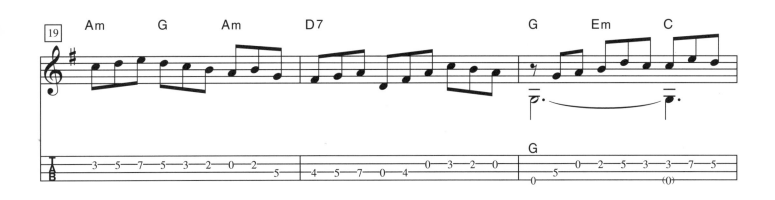

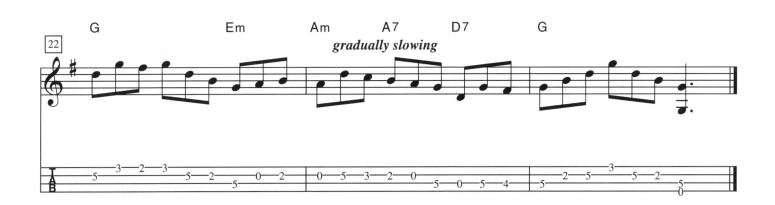

Serenade (Toselli)

For many years this famous Italian serenade was used as the theme song for a radio program called "The Goldbergs," the trials and tribulations of a poor Jewish family in 1930s New York City. Play this arrangement with a pretty tone and plenty of tremolo. Let the melody sing out, and don't play the time too strictly.

Enrico Toselli

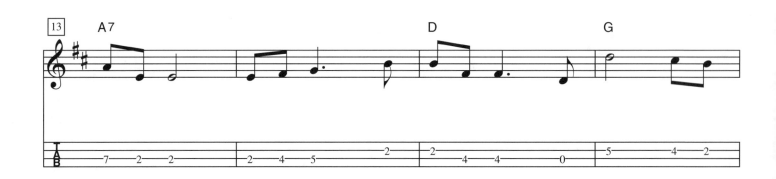

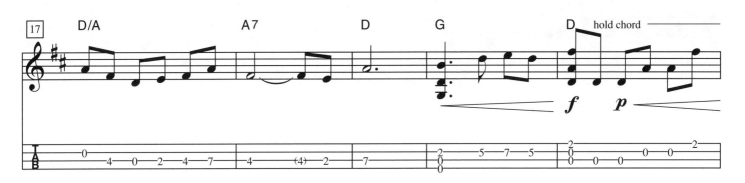

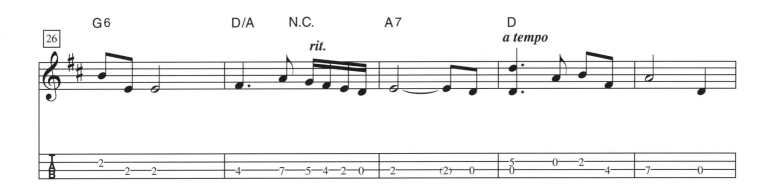

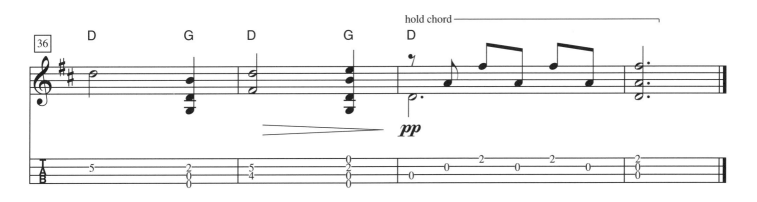

Plaisir d'Amour

The title means "The Pleasures of Love." Martini was an 18th-century Italian composer noted for his lovely melodies. This famous one was the basis for an Elvis Presley hit. Use a full tone and tremolo to bring out the beauty of the melody.

Padre Martini

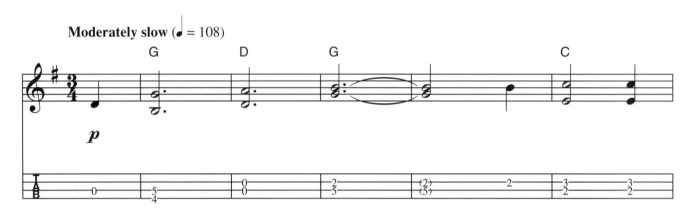

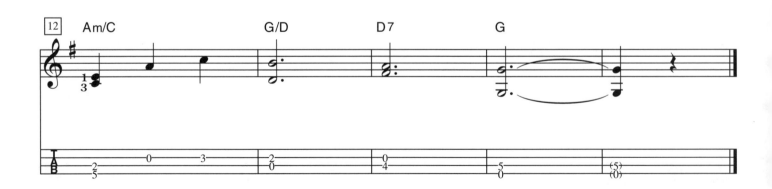

Serenade (Drigo)

This is one of the most famous melodies ever composed for the mandolin. Concentrate on tone and phrasing, and use tremolo on longer notes. Descending grace notes, such as in measure 9, can be played as pull-offs. Double grace-notes, such as in measure 21, should be played as a hammer-on followed by a pull-off.

Riccardo Drigo

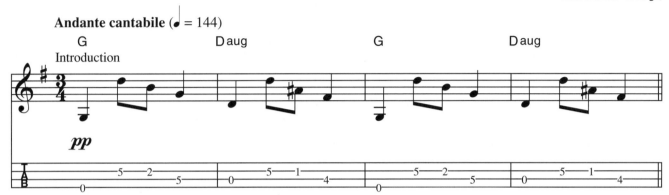

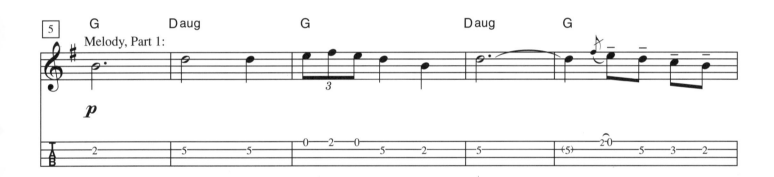

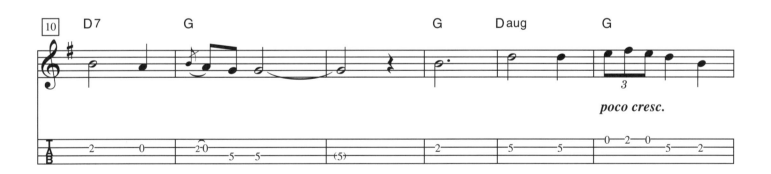

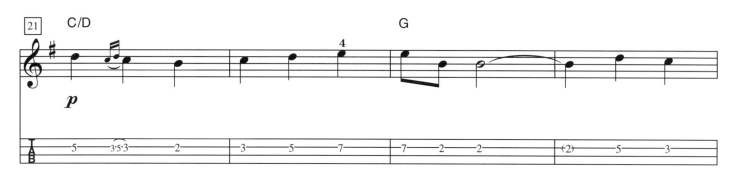

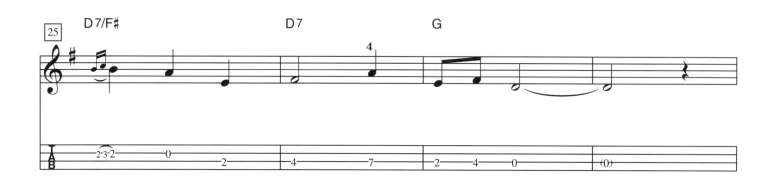

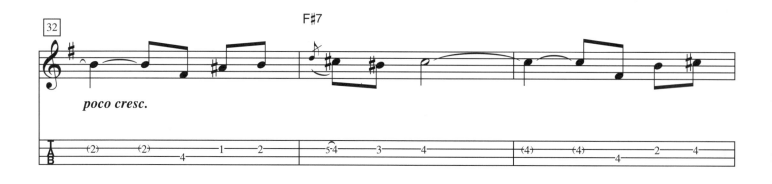

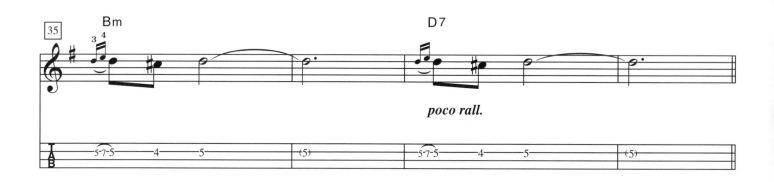

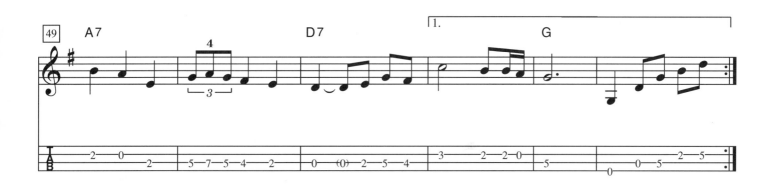

Canzonetta from Act II of Don Giovanni

During the early days of the mandolin, Mozart wrote this as the accompaniment to an aria sung by the incurable womanizer, Don Giovanni (also known as Don Juan), in the eponymous opera. In real life the Don would have played a pandura or other small fretted instrument because at the time the story takes place, the mandolin had not yet been invented.

W. A. Mozart
Edited by Dan Fox

Concerto in C Major

This is the complete solo mandolin part to this most famous of all classical pieces written for the mandolin. The main theme of the first movement became well known after it was used in the 1979 movie "Kramer vs. Kramer." Follow the fingering carefully and avoid using tremolo for an authentic performance; it was not used during the Baroque period when Vivaldi was composing.

Antonio Vivaldi
Edited by Dan Fox

1st Movement

2nd Movement

3rd Movement

Categorical Index

Alphabetical Index

Guitar Chord Charts

These solos (with the exception of the Vivaldi concerto and the Mozart canzonetta) can be played as duets using guitar accompaniment. The following diagrams show guitar fingering for every chord used in this book:

Major Chords

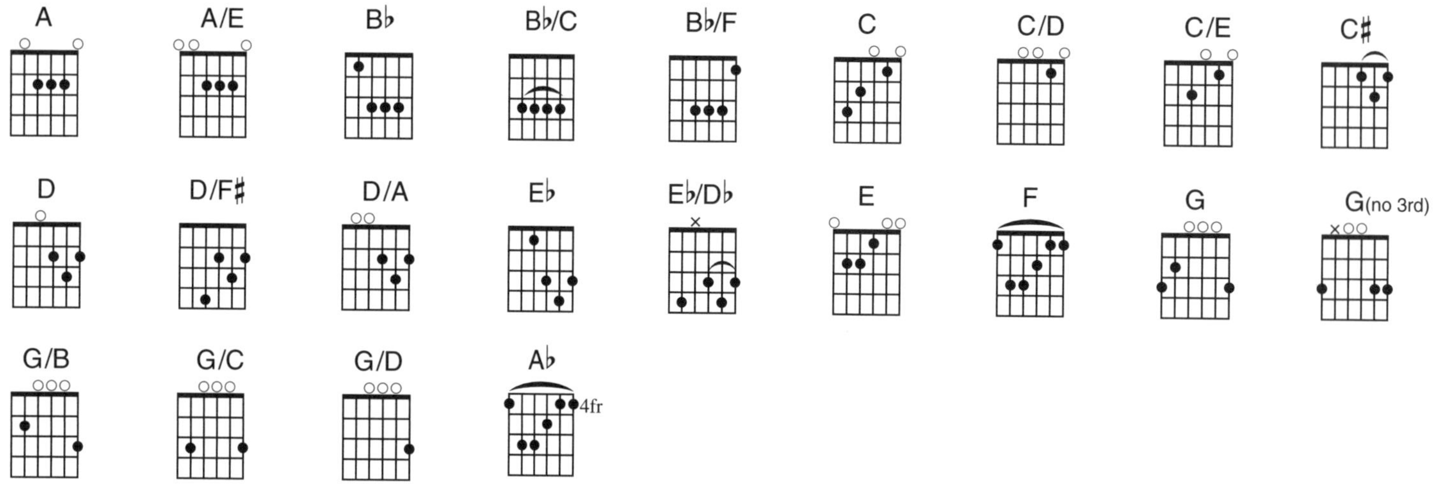

A   A/E   Bb   Bb/C   Bb/F   C   C/D   C/E   C#

D   D/F#   D/A   Eb   Eb/Db   E   F   G   G(no 3rd)

G/B   G/C   G/D   Ab

Minor Chords

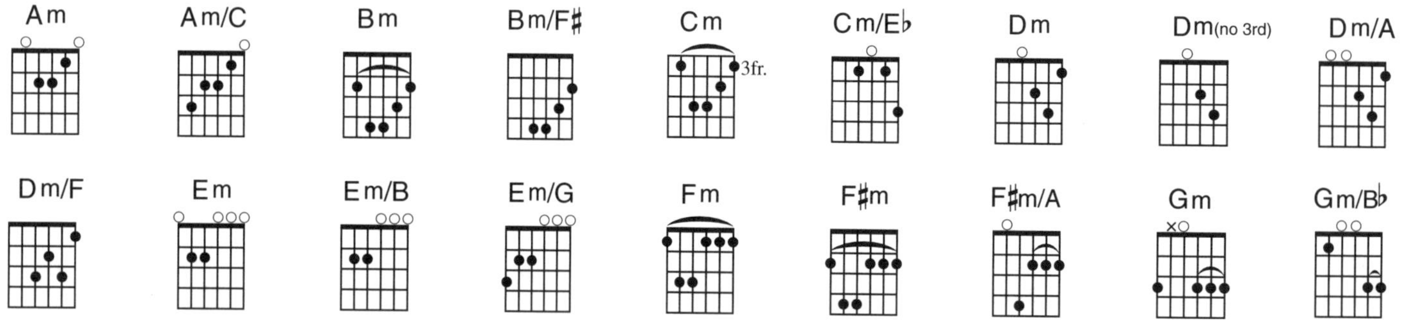

Am   Am/C   Bm   Bm/F#   Cm   Cm/Eb   Dm   Dm(no 3rd)   Dm/A

Dm/F   Em   Em/B   Em/G   Fm   F#m   F#m/A   Gm   Gm/Bb

Seventh Chords

A7   B7   C7   C#7   D7   D7/F#   Eb7   E7   F7

F#7   G7

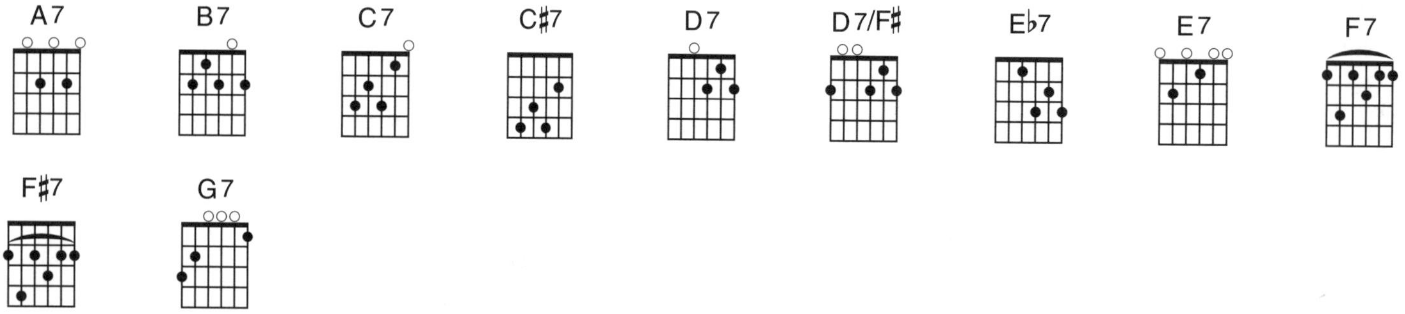

Other Chords

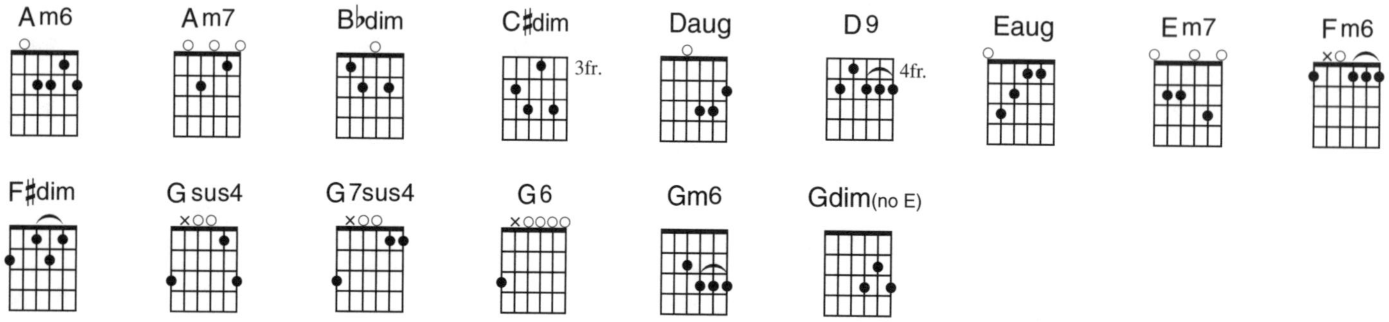

Am6   Am7   Bbdim   C#dim   Daug   D9   Eaug   Em7   Fm6

F#dim   Gsus4   G7sus4   G6   Gm6   Gdim(no E)

Mandolin Chord Charts

These solos (with the exception of the Vivaldi concerto and the Mozart canzonetta) can be played as duets using a second mandolin for accompaniment. The following diagrams show mandolin fingering for every chord used in this book:

Important: Mandolinists should ignore anything that follows a slash mark (/) after a chord symbol. For example, C/G should be played as C. D7/F♯ should be played as D7, etc. (C/G means to play a C chord with G in the bass. Since the mandolin has no bass notes to speak of, these can be safely ignored. However, guitarists, bassists and players of other instruments capable of playing bass notes find these symbols very important.)

Major Chords

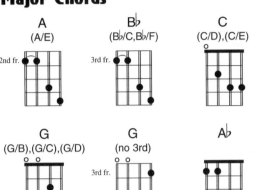
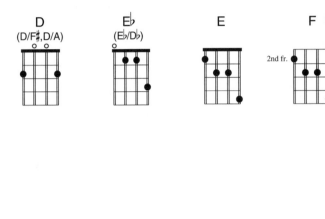

Minor Chords

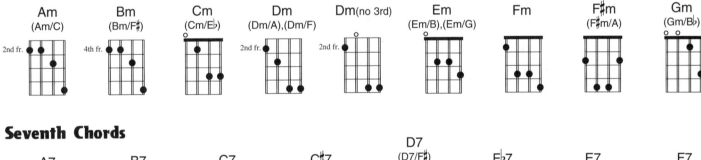

Seventh Chords

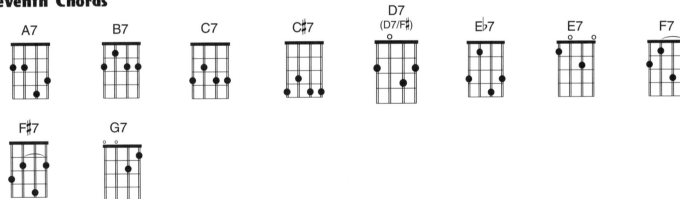

Other Chords

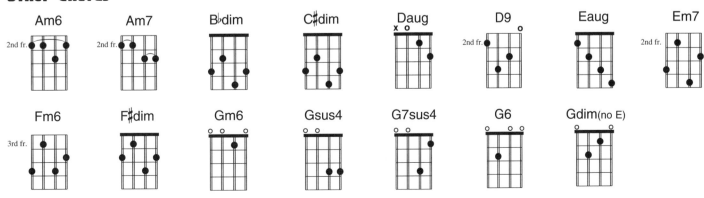

Tremolo

Because the mandolin cannot sustain notes the way a brass, woodwind, or bowed string instrument can, mandolinists use a technique called *tremolo* (TREM-uh-low) to sustain long notes. This is a rapid down-and-up picking across one or more strings. In this way the sound of a note or chord can be sustained indefinitely.

A smooth tremolo is one of the marks of a good mandolin player. It takes a fair amount of work to develop the nerves and muscles needed to produce it. Here's an exercise routine that will help develop a good tremolo. Set your metronome to a slow tempo, such as 60 beats-per-minute.

Ex. 1

Play a G major scale in quarter notes.

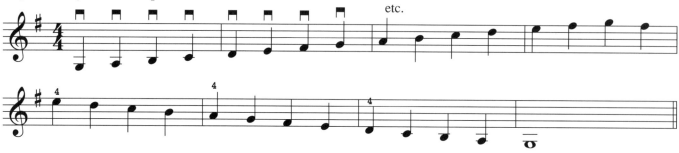

Ex. 2

Then play the scale as eighth notes, with a down-and-up pick on each scale step.

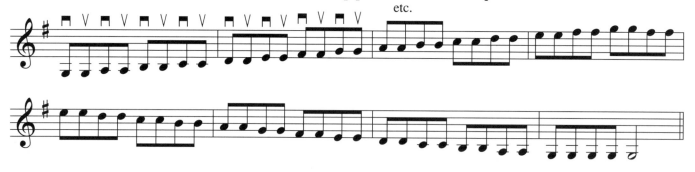

Ex. 3

Finally, play each scale step as four 16th notes.

Strive for a smooth, even tone. Keep the left-hand fingers down firmly; keep the right wrist relaxed, and don't grip the pick too tightly. When you can do these exercises flawlessly at 60 beats-per-minute, gradually increase the speed each day until you reach 160 beats-per-minute or the limit of your capabilities. The faster you can play the tremolo, the smoother and more beautiful it will sound. Practice your tremolo every day for best results.

The question of when to use this effect is largely a matter of taste. In general, use a lot of tremolo on Italian, Russian, Jewish and other ethnic songs, but only occasionally in bluegrass, and never in music written before 1800, because this effect was not used prior to the 19th century. Many of the arrangements have indications of when to tremolo, but these are suggestions only.

Tablature (TAB)

Tablature is a type of notation that developed as early as the 15th century. It is often used for fretted instruments such as guitar, banjo, and mandolin to indicate the position of a written note on the fingerboard. Mandolin tablature uses a four-line staff representing each double-string as one line of the TAB. A "0" on the lowest line means to play the G string open. A "2"

on the top line means play the 2nd fret on the E string, and so on. Please note that numbers on the TAB stand for frets, not fingers. When needed, fingering numbers are placed next to the applicable notes. In this book we have supplied tablature for every arrangement except for a few of the classical pieces.

Tempo

Tempo (the speed at which an arrangement is to be played) is indicated in two ways. First is a descriptive word or words such as "slowly," "brightly," "with spirit." The second is a quarter note, half note or eighth note followed by a number such as ♩ =112, or ♩ =72. This tells you which note gets the beat, and how many beats to play per minute. However, these are only suggested tempos. Your taste may dictate playing slower or faster.

Principles of Fingering

The following chart shows the names and usual fingering of the basic notes on the mandolin. The tablature shows the fret where each note is found on the fingerboard. However, some pieces call for alternative fingerings. These are marked on the individual arrangements.

Notes on the 4th string (G string)

Notes on the 3rd string (D string)

Notes on the 2nd string (A string)

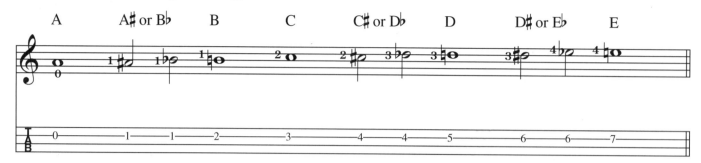

Notes on the 1st string (E string)

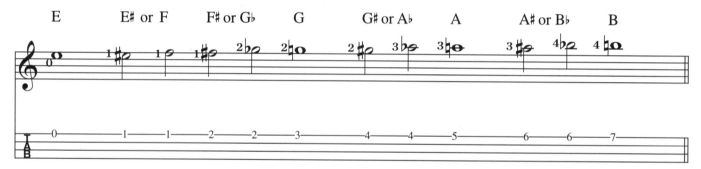

High notes on the 1st string (E string)

Note: The mandolin can be played all the way to double-high C, but unless you have an extremely fine instrument, the notes above high G tend to have an unsatisfactory tone quality.